D0939933

How to Dress Well: A Complete Guide for Women

Priscilla Hecht Grumet

Photographs by Bernard G. Cohen

CORNERSTONE LIBRARY
Published by Simon & Schuster, NEW YORK

Reprinted 1981

Published by Cornerstone Library,
A Simon & Schuster Division of
Gulf & Western Corporation
Simon & Schuster Building
Rockefeller Center
1230 Avenue of the Americas
New York, New York 10020

Designed by Stanley S. Drate

Manufactured in the United States of America
10 9 8 7 6 5 4 3 2 1

Picture Sources: Ph. Lédru-Sygma, 12; Wide World, 12; United
Press International, 13, 14, 15; Edward Carroll, 15.

Illustrations by Miriam Quervedo Graham

Library of Congress Cataloging in Publication Data

Grumet, Priscilla Hecht.
How to Dress Well: A Complete Guide for Women

Includes index.
I. Clothing and dress. I. Cohen, Bernard G. II. Title.
TT507.G78 646'.34 79-17135

ISBN 0-346-12510-3

to dear Ross,
my husband,
one summer night this book became our *book*

Contents

The Store

Foreword

The pace of progress in the past hundred years is nowhere more dizzyingly evident than in retailing. Just a century or so ago, itinerant peddlers bartered their wares through the countryside, while tradesmen offered townspeople what goods they could from market stalls or one-room general stores. The best of the latter became legend, growing into today's mercantile giants, selling more merchandise in a single morning than their founders ever dreamed existed. All that in just one store — most major retailers operate upwards of a score apiece — each competing fiercely in vast suburban malls or downtown shopping districts with other equally skilled and determined merchants for your shopping dollar.

The effects of this headlong rush into modern merchandising have the greatest impact on the customer and undoubtedly are most keenly felt as she shops for apparel. Looking for a dress, today's customer is confronted with a dozen, or two dozen, or five dozen decisions in the course of her shopping. As the makers of fibers, fabrics, and apparel have burgeoned apace with sellers, exactly the same variety and quantity that makes possible the unprecedented use of fashion as a creative medium of self-expression, also makes it discouragingly confusing. In addition, self-expression in the face of this plethora of fashion alternatives necessitates skillful self-assessment, a more than casual ability to filter and interpret the possibilities to achieve a well-orchestrated personal theme. Without bankrupting oneself in the process.

Priscilla Grumet's book addresses these problems — most realistically and broadly and understandably — and therein lies its value.

I like to think that Priscilla acquired much of her considerable fashion expertise during her tenure as a buyer for Rich's; certainly she displayed it here, to the benefit of customer and store alike. That expertise is clearly reflected in her refreshing departure from stereotyped theories about who can wear what, and why. Her understanding of the times of a woman's life, and the requirements of her changing lifestyles, is down to earth and completely pragmatic, as are her recommendations for obtaining the best value for every fashion dollar.

Every woman interested in looking her best, with a minimum of wasted time and money, will profit by the insights Priscilla provides in this book. Her warmth and humor will provoke an understanding smile from every shopper who has ever confronted truth in a three-way mirror.

Joel Goldberg

Chairman of the Executive Committee
Rich's
Atlanta, Georgia

Preface

I don't know whether it was genetics or environment that caused me to develop a love and understanding for fashion and merchandising. My father, who merchandised men's wear, said that I asked for a better style of silver spoon. And my maternal grandfather (also in merchandising: Buicks) added that I was not one to be satisfied with basic silver. Neither of them encouraged me directly to persist in my interest, but each enjoyed recounting the challenges of his chosen profession.

On second thought — was it in spite of, or because of, my mother's persistent critical reminders about how she wanted me to look, or what was the right way to look, that I became more introspective and autonomous, challenging myself to self-interpretation and self-expression? Growing up in the provincial South — Birmingham, Alabama — somehow stimulated my desire for self-expression. I found that clothes could be significant tools for defining my individuality.

I began working at thirteen after school and summers in small ready-to-wear stores. I was so stimulated by merchandising and selling that later, when I became a student at Stephens College, I indulged myself with every available related course and set as my goal upon graduating a job with a major department store. I spent the next seven years with Rich's Inc., one of the country's most exciting retail operations. Encouraged by my boss to think that my talents had no limits, I developed self-confidence and quickly implemented some original ideas. Rich's encouraged young thinkers. My functions involved buying, advertising, managing a department, customer service, and selling.

As my life evolved in the field of fashion, I expanded my interests and goals. I have taught the subject in fashion schools and at Emory University where my course, "The Psychology of Fashion," was attended by several hundred women. I have spoken to large and small groups and have reached other audiences through radio, television, and magazine interviews and through a fashion column, "Personally, Priscilla."

My friends often relied on my fashion knowledge. They'd bombard me with questions, especially when they went shopping. Once when one of my friends was marrying, she asked me to help her select her new wardrobe. At the end of a day's shopping spree, I returned home exhausted. After talking it over with my husband, I decided to charge for my services and the next day I was in business with my personal shopping service, which is now in its fourth year.

I have written this book because to my knowledge no other book like it is available for women. After working with women of all ages, I understand their problems. I am more and more convinced that most women have only a minimal knowledge of how to shop, where to shop, what to buy, and how to spend money wisely. More importantly, a great many women don't know what steps to take to achieve a more positive and attractive projection of themselves. I am keenly aware of the increasing variety of roles women play today and of the difficulties they have in looking good consistently in these various activities. Women do wish to look their best, but many do not know how. "I know what I like" and "I know what . . . (friend, relative, boss, authoritative source) likes" are usually statements indicative of impending fashion disaster.

This book is not written for high-fashion information purposes. On the contrary, it aims at the fashions and ideas of daily living — day and night, work, home, and travel. Women are in the midst of new life passages. They have taken on new responsibilities and have added new dimensions to their lives. They have more interest in themselves, but less time to devote to themselves. Here I explain how they can experiment with their looks and their individuality and how they can plan, shop for, and coordinate their wardrobes. I teach them to understand the clothes themselves and how to benefit from retailers and their services.

My commitment is to women, to their femininity, their assertiveness, their totality.

About the Photography. To see yourself, to see others, and to know how others see you—these are not spectator functions, but active skills of introspection. The photographs throughout this book differ in aim from photographs of high fashion or of models posing to display a particular garment. Instead, I have chosen to show women in their natural environments, hoping you will be moved to participate, to project yourself into their situations, and to ask yourself what makes them dress that way.

Acknowledgments

To Elizabeth Runyan and Doug Slavin, who shared, encouraged, and understood my metamorphosis, thank you for being part of my life for so many years.

To Paul Bonner, Jr., Madelyn Larsen, and Jane Wilson, who believed in me and in this book, and to Polly Fraser for her continued support and illustrative contributions, I shall always be grateful.

And to each of the following, who gave time, expertise, and friendship, my special thanks.

Ralph Baker; Anne P. Berg, Rich's, Inc.; Mary Cobb Bugg, Emory University; Patty Cerny, Saks Fifth Avenue, Atlanta; Sue Coates; Marilyn Cole; Scott Cole; Bernard Cohen; Marvin B. Cohen, President, Atlanta Handbag Co., Inc.; Robert Crow, M.D., P.C.; Bill Davis, Standard Club, P.G.A. Professional; Icola Davis, Saks Fifth Avenue, Atlanta; Martin Dubler, l8K, Inc.; H. Jay Epstein, Sea Dreams by Maidenform, Inc.; Dorothy K. Fierst, Peachtree Plaza Hotel, Atlanta; Polly Fraser; Jerry Gershonoff, President, Skippy Musket & Company; Helen Hecht; Naomi Kasper; Krazz, Atlanta Disco; Morris Brothers Luggage, Atlanta; Karen McNeill, Women's Wear Daily, Atlanta; Patricia Oliver, Charles Jourdan Boutique, Atlanta; Mary M. Patton, President, Haute Couture So., Inc., D/B/A Valentino Boutique; Rich's, Inc., Atlanta; Adria Spielberger; Bobbie C. Stelling; Peter J. Stelling, Vice President, George Muse Company; Jules J. Stine, President, A. J. Stine, Inc.; Tennis Lady, Atlanta; Barbara Weiss, Vice President, Snooty Hooty, Inc.

How to Dress Well:
A Complete Guide for Women

The language of dress prevails more than spoken language. Through clothes, styles, colors, and accessories (and how you wear them), you convey different messages simultaneously about your age, sex, occupation, beliefs, tastes, and mood.

The women in the following pages have made a positive statement about themselves.

Before you say a word, your appearance speaks. Not all women have a natural fashion flair. Decisions about dress take time and involve an awareness of our own self-image. Good taste and good style mean wearing the appropriate clothes for your figure and your personality.

The women in the following pages have not made a positive statement in their dress.

The Person

1

Clothes Make a Statement

If you want to make a statement about yourself, first decide which of your positive personal attributes to use.

At certain stages in your life, you may want to change your look from girlish to sophisticated, from classic to updated, from mature to more youthful.

No one can know better than you what you want to wear or how you want to look .

Mirror, Mirror on the Wall

I recall looking at Audrey Hepburn with envy. Her high cheek bones, narrow nose, and flat chest were features I knew I could never have, but nonetheless I wanted them. Perhaps my mirror should have been my enemy during those teenage years, but we became good friends. If I held my head upright and pushed back with my index finger, I could make the small bump on my nose temporarily disappear. I could also avoid looking at my profile. Flattening my chest was easier. I could either wear something loose fitting (I was only a C cup, and the loose fit surely brought me down to a B), or I could squeeze into a smaller, heavily elasticized bra and turn blue. We all played those games at seventeen, but the outcomes were never permanent and the next day I was back at the mirror inventing another chapter in the games Priscilla played.

Giving up the Audrey Hepburn body, my only hope was to emulate the Audrey Hepburn style. I watched her carefully and was able to pick out some things that could feasibly become part of me. She has the knack of varying her looks from classic to sexy to sophisticated, and I learned over the years how to make these statements in my own language rather than in hers.

If you want to make a statement about yourself, first decide which of your positive physical attributes to use. Also consider whether you prefer to be innovative (and conspicuous) or conservative (and less obvious). These decisions and their implementation must involve self-examination and time. Begin slowly and experiment.

Often it is easiest to try something new at home. One of my students, a woman in her mid-thirties, made most of us envious in a recent class by describing how, since her first year in college, she arranged her weekly schedule with an "off day." Between the hours of 10 A.M. and 3 P.M. she experimented with make-up samples she had collected from store cosmetic departments, changed the color of her hair with rinse-out tint, and modeled in front of her mirror in clothes she hadn't worn for a long time or those she had recently bought. Often she would share these experiments and new looks with her family and friends.

This kind of gradual self-exposure is the best way to obtain confidence with ease.

A Foolish Consistency

Do not rush into making dress decisions. Your decision may be *not* to wear something rather than to wear it, with a resulting increase in comfort and confidence. You will feel better dressed in what is comfortable for you. Experimentation is necessary. There is no reason to be absolutely consistent in your dress. A cross between Sophia Loren and Billy Jean King may be exactly what you're looking for. Instead of trying to figure out what others might like, permit yourself to explore your own personal dimensions. Don't boggle your mind with a monolithic or oversimplified identity problem. Women's lifestyles today are varied and eclectic. Your fashion objective is to work out a complete look from various composites, and to be your own woman.

A woman with a career might want to dress stylishly and assertively while on the job, but be more feminine at night. The same principle would apply to the woman whose day centers on her family and community, but who prefers a more provocative self in other situations. It is possible that you may be looking for a new or changed self-image. At certain stages or passages in your life, you may want to change your look from girlish to sophisticated, from classic to updated, from mature to more youthful.

Silence Is Golden

Look in the mirror before you leave home or office and before attending any business or social function, to check your clothing, hair, and make-up. You will feel much more at ease and certain about yourself. Most importantly, do not rush when dressing. Give yourself ample time to enjoy putting on make-up, combing your hair, and experimenting with your clothes. A last-minute change in coordinates and accessories often is needed and this takes time. When possible, dress in a room that has good light and is quiet. Time is limited, and time free from noise and outside pressure can become impossible unless you make a firm commitment to yourself. Why not invoke a knock-before-entering policy? Kids do. Otherwise, we are dressing to the cacophonous sounds of children's demands, Donnie and Marie's latest release, and the ringing of the telephone.

When you are dressing, you should be calm.

Professionally Speaking

Before you say a word, your appearance speaks. What a woman looks like and what she does with her looks is totally up to her. Your look should be a manifestation of your individuality. No one can know better than you what you want to wear or how you want to look. Every woman does not have a natural fashion flair. Every woman can learn from professionals and from observation how to express her uniqueness in the vocabulary of fashion. In our culture, what you wear is a significant element in your self-definition. We are taught to value individuality. Therefore, your clothes should give the impression of being made for you alone. If your clothes are consistent with your own sense of personality, a feeling of security and wholeness results.

Pat, Jackie, and Rosalyn

What you wear and how you look amount to a statement. Think of Pat Nixon, who dressed with taste but whose clothes said little about her. Is this why many people thought of her as lacking a distinct personality? Her clothes were neat and well-tailored, but they had no flair and made no clear statement. We don't remember what she wore, or who she said she was, or what her beliefs were. Jackie Kennedy, on the other hand, achieved an immediate personal identity. We believed she was her own woman and today she remains a woman of style. Jackie wore pants everywhere, before many of us

How you look is a statement. Pat Nixon's clothes said little about her. Is this why many people thought of her as lacking a distinctive personality? What is individual about her here?

Jackie Kennedy achieved an immediate personal identity. Each of her gowns individually may not be remembered, but the looks they portrayed have been retained in current styles. (1977)

wore pants anywhere, before pants took priority over all other looks in all women's wardrobes. Pants have become an acceptable dress in almost every situation. Jackie Kennedy developed a style of chiseled simplicity for various moods and occasions. At night her clothes were elegant statements of sophisticated demeanor. Each of her gowns may not be remembered individually, but the looks they portrayed have been retained in current styles. While displeasing the fashion industry, Rosalyn Carter exposed her strong convictions. She chose to wear to the president's inaugural ball the same blue gown that she wore years earlier to Jimmy Carter's gubernatorial ball.

The expression of personality through clothes and appearance is what fashion is all about. Fashion is not discovering and imitating the clothes of celebrities and models. True fashion is creative and results from the interaction between your inner self and available materials.

Her Hat, Her Navel, Her Wig

Does your image just happen or is it created? Well-known women in the world are usually remembered by the words, clothes, or special trademarks associated with them. These characteristics become a part of them each time they are in the public eye. It even leads to absurdities: do we think of Bella Abzug sleeping with her hat on? Whether you recall her name or not, you think of her as the hat-wearing former congresswoman from New York City.

Well-known women can be remembered by their trademarks. Bella Abzug may be recalled as the hat-wearing former congresswoman from New York.

Special characteristics are associated with certain women each time they are in the public eye. It even leads to absurdities. Dolly Parton believes her extravagant wigs have helped her to singing fame.

Dolly Parton believes her extravagant wigs have helped bring her singing fame, and Bob Mackie is credited with making Cher's navel a television phenomenon. Burton Miller, Hollywood designer, believes dramatic, flamboyant, and unusual clothes create memorable impact. It may take months of thinking, planning, and experimenting to achieve this, but the result is a person who gives the impression of being unique in personality and dress.

Style

Style in general, as well as style in costuming, is perfected by the same methods I used in my adolescent emulation of Audrey Hepburn. Style means the way a person takes an existing item or trend and makes it characteristic and uniquely personal to themselves. No woman is born with style. Perhaps Lena Horne, Bess Meyerson, and Arlene Francis learned it from their mothers, but probably they acquired their images over a number of years. Arlene Francis may always wear her diamond heart for sentimental reasons, but when we see her we see the heart around her neck, too. She is able to wear this in good taste and it does not become flamboyant. Good taste and good style mean wearing the appropriate clothes for your figure and your personality, and wearing them at the appropriate times. You may look your best in blue jeans, feel your best and enjoy them more than anything else you wear, but even if they are appropriate for your daytime job or leisure they will be inappropriate for a formal dinner. Your dress option in this case might be to buy a pair of pants styled like jeans but made of soft velvet and worn with a jacket.

No woman is born with style. Perhaps Lena Horne learned it from her mother, but probably she acquired her image over a number of years.

Arlene Francis may always wear her diamond heart for sentimental reasons, but when we see her we see the heart around her neck too.

A Fad

Fads are temporary fashions that come and go quickly. Now and then, after a fad simmers down, it develops into a classic. Penny loafers are an example of this. They were a must during my high school days; since then they have faded as a fad (though they emerge periodically in new fabrics and colors). Penny loafers now are classics.

Be cautious when you invest in a fad, since it may not look good on you and may be a costly purchase for a very short wearing time. Some fad items, such as scarves or belts of a certain style, are less costly investments and they can be fun. Style fads create more problems than fabric and color fads. The latter can be incorporated into another season by blending, contrasting, or layering them with new and old styles, to become your new statement for the season.

Clothes Speak

The language of dress in our country prevails more than spoken language. Regardless of nationality, we all wear clothes and all clothes speak. Using the language of dress, individual speakers employ subtle or overt variations. Your vocabulary contains not only the clothes, with their styles, colors, and accessories, but also the way you wear them (your personal accent or interpretation). For those with a limited wardrobe, some practical considerations are comfort, care, durability, availability, and price. You convey different messages simultaneously about your age, sex, occupation, beliefs, tastes, and moods. You may choose to "speak" with classic clothes (a blazer), but also enjoy very contemporary conversation with jewelry (diamonds by the yard). A "fashion leader" expresses herself with several hundred items, while the dress vocabulary of a rural farmer may be extremely limited.

Be aware that clothes can give out misinformation. On several occasions in different cities I have worn obviously inexpensive jeans and a simple T-shirt while shopping. The salespeople in expensive shops were disinterested. Returning to the same store in fine clothes, I was treated differently. The blue jeans had told them that I could not afford expensive merchandise or that I had no style. People react to the language of dress often irreversibly. Had I chosen blue jeans that were detailed and looked expensive or had a designer label, and if the top had been a silk shirt, the message would have been different. The way you wear your clothes also speaks volumes.

Let's Talk Liberation

Liberation in dress is having choices and using them. Many girls' schools used to forbid pants as "unladylike." My college, in 1963, allowed pants only if the temperature was below freezing. In today's advertisements, the housewife is seen wearing pants rather than the conservative shirtdress, and dignified women of all economic levels wear pants. Pants have been considered vulgar if too tight, or masculine if too baggy, but now that pants have become an accepted style of dress for women there are fewer judgmental connotations.

Women have more options now to dress for their individual moods or circumstances. Moods may change. At times you want your clothes to appeal to one sex or the other. At a singles weekend you may want male attention, but at a morning tea you may prefer female attention. There are also times when you want the attention of both sexes, as in business or community meetings. Some modes of dress speak more loudly to women than to men, and vice versa. If you choose a sheer voile camisole revealing a bare breast underneath, men would react sexually, some positively (liking it), others negatively (too revealing for them). And some men would not like that look on a woman they were with. A woman's reaction could be one of interest, or of threat and competition. The same camisole worn with an undergarment would probably receive no reaction one way or the other from either sex.

Choose Comfort

I will repeat throughout this book the importance of being comfortable in whatever you are wearing. Regardless of how good you might look, if what you are wearing is not a comfortable style you will not feel self-confident and you will convey this. Though I think that shoes with very high heels look "sexy", my feet are uncomfortable in them, and even if my goal was to attract male attention, I would not wear them. Do not wear a style that will make you uneasy.

The word "sexy" has a narrow meaning, and I will therefore also use the word "appeal" in discussing broader ideas about dress selections that have significance for men. Not only what you wear, but how you wear it is significant. For instance, a satin or silk shirt which buttons up the front can be classic with only the top button left open, or it can have great sex appeal, when the top three buttons are left unbuttoned to reveal the breast, especially when you move.

Appealing to Him

Fabrics should give a touchable impression: silk, satin, velvet, suede, or cashmere.

Color should talk, say something, but it should not scream. Pastels — soft blues, pinks, yellows or bolds — red, black, purple. Keep your patterns to a minimum, they needn't jump out.

Fabric and color choice should encourage a man to come closer to you and observe you. Textures should be interesting and ask for attention. If you have never been fully aware of fabric or texture reactions, go to a fabric shop to feel the different fabrics and be aware of your own reactions. Does the fabric feel soft and touchable or does it feel cold and harsh? Your own reaction will be a good guide.

Make sure the *fit* is good. Let your clothes hug your body. Too tight or too loose will be equally unappealing. Never wear anything that is in need of repair. Broken zippers, lost buttons, and pinned waistlines are sure turn-offs.

Styles can include sweaters with cowl necks that fall softly, or turtle necks that fit snugly in soft wool or cashmere, but not bulky sweaters that cover up the shape of the body. Crochet and loose weaves both have positive appeal. Necklines may be off the shoulder, low, or with button fronts (which you will wear partly unbuttoned). Add pants, jeans, or skirts depending upon the occasion. Skirts and pants should either fit snugly, showing the contour of the body, or be soft and flowing, showing movement. Very full or high-styled garments produce female interest rather than male attraction. Remember to keep the styling simple: halters, V necklines, off-the-shoulder or backless styles, low fronts, shirtdresses with three buttons unbuttoned, all create positive appeal to men.

Accessories

In choosing your accessories, think of additions that would be eye-catching, or those that would be touchable, such as furs, feathers, and sculptured beads. Also consider those that encourage conversation, such as unusual jewelry designs, something you have made or have bought while traveling in another country.

Shoes and purses should never be heavy or bulky. A high-heeled open sandal or a rich leather or suede contoured boot are good choices.

Remember to be comfortable. Wear the same things often if you feel good in them. Don't overdress with too much jewelry or too many layers of clothing. Select the styles that look best on you, and only choose things that are "in" this year if they also look good on you. There are enough alternative choices available to enhance your personal positives.

Appealing to Her

A woman's reaction to other women's clothes is more critical than a man's reaction. A woman can be pleased to be in the company of another well-dressed woman, or she can feel threatened and insecure. Your clothes should make you feel good about yourself regardless of another person's response. To accomplish this goal, dress with style rather than flamboyance. Don't be overdressed or competitive in your clothes. Whether the situation is social or business, let your personality come first rather than your clothes. Wear well-tailored clothes and coordinate your complete look (see Chapter 2, *Your Life*, for more specifics.)

2

Your Life

If you are making some significant life changes, you may need to think of a new approach to your wardrobe.

The only way an employer knows you are serious about wanting a job is if you say so, and your clothes must be part of this statement.

There are certain advantages to reaching a certain age. You become more sure of yourself and this reflects in your clothes.

There seem to be swings in fashion from relative freedom to relative authoritarianism. Usually, as now, we are somewhere in the middle. No one today can dictate what is right or wrong in fashion. Nor is it a time like the recent past, when anything seemed right, at any time. Though blue jeans might be your favorite wardrobe item, you have settled down to wearing them only some of the time. Several years ago, at the height of the jean phenomenon, I got up each morning to find the same pair of jeans I had taken off the night before, thrown on the same chair, staring me in the face. For days I enjoyed the decisionless ease and comfort of wearing them everywhere except to bed. But I reached a mysterious limit one day, stared at those jeans and thought, "My God, they know my schedule better than I do." I looked in the mirror and decided that's it, I've had enough. I wear them often now, but I incorporate them into my wardrobe depending upon my schedule. I don't think I will ever give them up.

Your life's schedule does change, so your wardrobe must be flexible. If you are making some significant life changes, you may need to think of a new approach to your wardrobe. You may be planning to enter the job market and will need clothes for interviews and for work. Perhaps you no longer have a job but are active with community work and entertaining at home. Before you shop, you must take a complete look at your wardrobe and decide how to plan new purchases that will blend with the clothes you already have. It is not necessary to start anew. Clothes you now enjoy wearing can either be coordinated with something new or accessorized differently to function differently. A black skirt that you have been wearing to the office with silk shirts can now be worn with a mohair bulky sweater to the night class you are taking on a college campus. The gray flannel jacket you wear with jeans to shop for groceries will instead be perfect to go over a gray tweed dress you will buy for the office. The following pages will give you more detailed suggestions for your specific lifestyle.

Yes, I Want a Job

The only way an employer knows you are serious about wanting a job is if you say so, and your clothes must be part of this statement. You cannot be positive in your approach unless you feel this way about yourself and tell yourself so by the way you dress.

If you are new to going on interviews, here are some points to remember. Try to schedule your most important appointments at midmorning, not too early, so you have time enough to groom yourself without being rushed. Take time for that extra cup of coffee, go over your make-up and hair slowly, and give yourself plenty of travel time. Never rush! If your appointments are late in the day, you may be nervous waiting or tired from other pressures, and your make-up and clothes will not be as fresh.

Be absolutely certain that whatever you wear is comfortable. If some of what you are wearing is new, it is best to try your complete outfit on at home and wear it for several hours. Keep the temperature in mind; do not choose anything heavy to wear in a warm office, since you may spend time waiting for your interview, and though it might be cold outside you will perspire inside. Don't be too bare, lest the air conditioning be excessive. Be wary of coats that are difficult to unbutton; you should want to feel relaxed. (The coat I bought recently is marvelous to look at but takes at least five minutes to button and unbutton, which is a nuisance when I have a business appointment.) Are your leather gloves easy to remove? You will be taking them off many times during the day. Are your shoes comfortable? You may do a lot of walking and standing in line, so don't wear a pair that you have not broken in. You cannot do well in an interview if you are in pain.

How do your clothes look after sitting and standing in them for several hours? It's better to experiment at home rather than risk unexpected discoveries while waiting to be interviewed. Some fabrics (linen, silk, cotton) do not pass the wrinkle test. Pants often wrinkle quickly over the abdomen and thighs, so select wool or blended fabric pants that are less apt to show wrinkles. Some clothes need constant attention if you are moving about: blouses must be tucked if they are not smooth-fitting, shawls adjusted, belts tied. Choose an outfit that is trouble-free, since during the interview you don't want to be putting yourself together.

Do not over-accessorize. Though a muffler may look right with your coat, it can become annoying each time you remove it and you may even forget and leave it behind. Wear simple jewelry, since some bracelets and rings are noisy or inconvenient when you write and others are bulky when you are shaking hands. Your purse should be functional and easy to open and close. This is also true if you carry a briefcase or portfolio. Be sure that your purse or briefcase is well organized, to avoid fumbling through your papers.

Exactly What Do You Wear?

The type of job you are being interviewed for makes a difference. Someone seeking an advertising job may be more creative in dress than someone seeking a job in a downtown law firm. However, good taste and quality are vital regardless of the job. There are regional differences, too. Those who work and live on the West Coast seem to wear more color than Easterners do. It is important not to disregard these conventions.

A basic interview rule is: *do not overdress*. Use flair and self-expression, but dress to reflect the job you are applying for. Consider whether you will be interviewed by a man or a woman. Do not dress competitively or risk unnecessary antagonism. Leave an expensive fur coat and jewelry at home. Don't look too frilly or too sexy; save your evening shoes and dress for dancing. Whatever you decide to wear, it must be neat. Avoid elaborate make-up, jewelry, and overelaborate hair styles.

SOME INTERVIEW "LOOKS"

Classic

Navy blue blazer, wool or lightweight, depending upon the climate
Powder-blue fitted silky shirt, or powder-blue cowl-neck sweater
Navy blue tweed skirt or pants (if they are tailored well)
Solid or tweed coat
Tailored pump, walking shoe, or boot in brown suede or leather

Leather or suede purse, not too large or bulky
Brown leather briefcase
Simple pearl, gold, or silver earrings, not too large
Strand of pearls, alone or combined with one or two chains
Two gold or silver bracelets
A stick pin or bar pin on blazer lapel
A belt is optional, brown suede or leather, with a simple buckle

Comfortable

Tan challis skirt and top, long- or short-sleeved
Small patterned challis jacket
Brown, tan, or camel leather pump or walking shoe
Brown, tan, or camel leather purse, not too large or bulky
Leather briefcase
Simple gold, wood, or tortoise-shell earrings, not too large
Gold or wood neckband combined with chains
Two bracelets — gold, tortoise-shell, or wood

Sophisticated

Gray wool tweed jumper
Mauve fitted silky shirt or cowl/turtleneck sweater
Solid gray or burgundy coat or cardigan sweater, long or short
Dark brown or black walking shoe or boot, leather or suede
Dark brown or black suede or leather purse, very tailored
Leather briefcase
Silver or pearl earrings, not too large
Lightweight silver chain, or strand of pearls at neckline with blouse
One or two small pins on neckline with sweater
Pearl and silver bracelets

Classic Chic

Black wool or challis skirt
Beige and black fitted shirt, small print
Solid black or beige sweater or jacket
Black or tan leather pump, walking shoe, or boot
Black or tan purse, not too large or bulky
Leather briefcase
Beige leather or suede belt
Thin gold necklace at neckline, one longer gold necklace
Small gold earrings
Two bracelets, gold, wood, or beads

Last-Minute Tidbits

Make it easy on yourself by being super-organized. Here are some last-minute suggestions:

Take along an extra pair of hose.

Extra make-up touch-ups may be needed during the day, so have your make-up with you in a separate pouch in your purse.

Bring a note pad and pen, since you will hope to have important information to write down.

Gloves are optional, less so in cold weather, but remove them when shaking hands.

If you wear a hat, it should be a part of your outfit and also look well with what you are wearing when your coat is removed.

Clothes on the Job

Don't rush out to refurbish your wardrobe the first week on the job. Go to work in clothes you feel comfortable in, and take several weeks to learn the flavor of what most people are wearing. As always, fashion means integrating your personal character with your environment. Do women wear pants here? Are jeans acceptable? Is the atmosphere very conservative? No, you don't want to dress exactly like the others, but neither do you want to be unusually different. You want to speak the same language but use your own words and ideas. Consider your comfort. Do you need sweaters in an office that sets a low thermostat? Will you be on your feet a lot? If so, you might always need a second pair of shoes with you. Will you be traveling? Is there good security for your personal belongings or a cabinet for coat and purse? Will you need to buy a briefcase? Buy additions to your working wardrobe slowly. Here are some other questions you should ask yourself before making new purchases:

What do I already have in my wardrobe that is suitable on the job? You may only need to add one new pair of shoes to an outfit to adapt it for working.

Is the fabric of this new skirt and blouse durable? Will it hold its shape after you sit in it for many hours?

Is the weight of the fabric too seasonal? Some fabrics (gabardine, crepe) will be appropriate most months in most climates; others will not give you this freedom.

Will you be purchasing a new coat or raincoat? Make sure it is easy to get on and off and is of a weight that will give you necessary warmth. Those with zip-out linings can be most functional.

Are the colors you are adding flexible within your wardrobe? (See Chapter 6, *Planning a Wardrobe.)*

The Job Makes a Difference

In addition to looking good, you also must select what is appropriate for the job. Many jobs require specific looks and items that function in a special way. Consider the following situations.

Your job may require entertaining in the evening if you are an insurance agent, newspaper reporter, or officer of a company, for example. You might select a wool skirt and jacket with a tailored shirt for daytime. This permits an easy change into a satin top for cocktails and dinner.

If you are in the real estate business and will be walking property, your shoes should be comfortable but not costly, since weather often may ruin them. Since you may be outside a lot, choose clothes that look well with jackets or sweaters. Be sure your coat is comfortable for driving.

If your job requires travel, fabric consideration is vital. Wool, crepe, and fabric blends require minimal care. You must be able to quickly coordinate your wardrobe, so separates are vital. One jacket or blazer in a neutral color will do to complete most of the outfits. Traveling requires a varied accessory wardrobe to change the looks of your basic clothes.

If your job requires contact with equipment and supplies (working with advertising, art, machinery), choose short-sleeved styles that will not soil easily; long sleeves can be damaged by ink or paint. Be cautious of buying clothes that require dry-cleaning. Perhaps you have the kind of job where dress can be less conservative. If so, jeans, boots, and more faddy clothes may be comfortable to work in, and they permit spontaneity or creativity. However, on days when you will be in business meetings or calling on conservative clients, you might eliminate the striped wool sweater in favor of a solid-color one.

If you work with children, regardless of their age, choose some clothes that will spark conversation, such as an interesting belt buckle, a patchwork jacket, unusual jewelry. Bright colors and textures interesting to touch can initiate responses. If you are working with young children or in areas where clothes will be soiled, choose fabrics that are easy to care for.

In all types of sales work you will be meeting the public. It is important that you present the images of your employer and the products that you sell. If you are selling art in an exclusive gallery, your dress should be chic, perhaps a beige wool crepe dress with a strand of pearls. If the art is avant-garde, satin paisley pants and shirt would be great. If you are selling fashion ready-to-wear, dress the part. Be very up-to-date and select clothes that present this image. If berets are fashionable that season, and if they look good on you, then wear them.

Jan Stephenson, professional golfer, believes that wearing an outfit she really likes gives her a psychological lift and enables her to play a better game. Polly Bergen likes the fun of dressing for her office in the morning, and later

Many jobs require specific looks. You might select a wool skirt and jacket for daytime. This permits an easy accessory change for cocktails and dinner. Shoes, scarf, and handbag do make a difference.

In various facets of your job, you may have the dress option of being faddy or conservative. Make the same outfit work either way, with accessory changes.

It is important that you present the image of your employer, and the products that you sell. The look in dress may vary from avant-garde (satin paisley pants) to chic (a beige wool dress).

in the day changing her accessories to show another part of her personality. Men enjoy the transformation of a woman from a strictly business presentation by day to a softer look at night. Allow your clothes to say many things, and give your purchases much thought. Remember your various roles and the things you want to say through fashion.

It's Not the Quantity That Counts

The clothes you choose as basics in your working wardrobe should be adaptable to a multitude of accessories. Scarves, shawls, jewelry, shoes, and belts will change your look easily, increasing and stretching your entire wardrobe. The number of accessories is less important than the flexibility of each piece. To integrate colors, keep them to a minimum (see Chapter 6, *Planning a Wardrobe*). Use magazines, advertisements, and other media as sources of fresh ideas. What you wear should make you feel good about what you are doing.

A Business Check List

You may need to make some specific purchases for your new job. Take time to comparison-shop, since styles and prices differ and some stores will have a larger stock of the item to choose from. Ask questions of the salespeople to assure a correct purchase.

The briefcase: It should be of good quality and have a business image. It can be leather, suede, or canvas with a leather or suede trim. A dark color will not show wear as much. Canvas is very durable. Make sure the briefcase is not too heavy; you might consider one of the newer soft cases. Those with compartments enable more organization. Handles and a shoulder strap are an advantage for easy maneuvering, and the bag must open and close easily. Some jobs require more than one briefcase, particularly jobs that involve travel. For a quality briefcase plan to spend at least $100.

The purse: For business use, your purse should be an investment in quality. Consider a good grade of leather. (Suede is nice but perishable.) A smart canvas purse is fine. Avoid plastic. Choose a neutral color: black, tan, or brown. The purse must be practical and easy to open and close. Don't select one so small that it always bulges, and suitcase-size is no better. Compartments are always an advantage, especially when you are traveling. Outside zipper pockets are great for those things you need in a hurry, such as airline tickets, keys, and pens. An individual make-up bag to carry in your purse is very helpful. An address book and a case for business cards usually are needed. Select quality ones.

In the Community and at Home

If you are active in your community — representing a group of people, volunteering for projects, taking an interest in your child's school — your dress is an important element of your role and should reflect both a business and a personal attitude. You probably don't want to give a bandbox appearance or be dowdy either. Soft or rich shades and subtle or small patterns are best. Consider a two-piece paisley challis skirt and top, a pearl-gray wool dress, or a navy flannel suit. These also can easily be incorporated into your leisure life, worn to luncheons, out to dinner, or for family travel. It is not necessary to have separate community and leisure wardrobes. However, it may require special effort to keep your clothes clean, neat, and up to date.

Your favorite clothes for wearing at home should not be worn away from the house. The torn jeans and faded shirt are strictly at-home work clothes. My philosophy is that wherever you are you should never have to say "I'm sorry." Why shouldn't you enjoy looking at yourself in the mirror, and why shouldn't family and friends see you looking good? Rid your closet of the has-beens; if they are not there you won't be tempted to wear them. Yes, you should be comfortable and relaxed in your at-home clothes and some loungewear is made just for that purpose. Without spending a lot of money you can look fresh and easy. For wearing at home or in your yard, there are zip-up jumpsuits in terrycloth, jersey, flannel, and other easy-care fabrics. They are suitable for apartment living (not Sutton Place, perhaps), getting your mail, walking the dog, or using central laundry facilities. Sandals, mules, and soft leather slippers can be both attractive and comfortable. If your make-up is fresh and you add a little jewelry (I wear earrings all the time, even to sleep), many at-home looks will be very suitable to wear for dinner guests.

Guess Who's Coming to Dinner?

When entertaining, be thoughtful about your dress, whether the occasion is evening for two, a dinner for many guests, or a family get-together. What you wear for him won't be exactly what you would wear for nieces and nephews, so you will need choices in your wardrobe. If you will be cooking or serving food, wear clothes that are comfortable and cool, because the kitchen will get warm. I would recommend not wearing a favorite outfit that could get splattered. However, aprons make great cover-ups and here you have an array of styles to choose from; long ones and short ones in colorful prints or solids are sold almost everywhere.

If you're having dinner for two, choose a soft jumpsuit in satin, jersey, silk, or terrycloth, or a hostess robe in a similar fabric. The wrap robe is a wonderful look, but almost all of them come open when you move. If you want to be that suggestive, fine, otherwise pick a zip-front or button-up. Caftans are some women's favorites, especially if you have a little excess weight to conceal. A great-looking pair of slacks with a silky or satin shirt is always positive. Remember to unbutton the first few buttons on shirts for a sexier look. When you're entertaining him, wear those soft, touchable fabrics. Accessorize with jewelry. Your shoes or slippers must be comfortable. Looking provocative or demure can be the right statement, but consider subtlety. For a dressier at-home look, buy a hostess gown with a V neckline, halter or strapless top, in silk, satin, lurex, or cashmere. Select one that can also be worn to dinner or to parties away from the house.

At Home and Away

In warm weather, two-piece loungewear is ideal for entertaining or relaxing. All colors and fabrics are available, and many of them can be worn as beach cover-ups too. I love terrycloth or jersey both at home and on vacation. Peasant and patio dresses worn with sandals can take you almost anywhere. Add a shawl, and you have two looks instead of one.

Your clothes for at-home entertaining should blend well with your furnishings. Choose colors and patterns that will enhance your surroundings and not detract from you or the place where you are.

Casually Speaking

Almost before I've shut the door behind me in the evening, I am out of the clothes I have been in all day. I want to be comfortable at home. However, I want to look pretty too. I have different robes and loungewear for my various moods. In winter weather nothing feels more right than a soft quilted robe. During the spring and summer, the patio is my favorite place for reading. The look of a full-length cotton T-shirt is ideal, great for cooking dinner and for those times when friends drop by unexpectedly. I like keeping my jewelry on, and my make-up is always fresh. I like to look good.

You've Come a Long Way

My attractive forty-five-year-old friend described the clothes she shops for now as seeming "more like liabilities than assets. Now that I can finally afford it, I feel I must buy better clothes and stay away from the faddish stuff. My college daughter says, adamantly, that mothers should not shop for their own clothes together with their daughters in the junior department. What a blow to the ego."

But does it have to be so? It's true that at certain ages some styles must go. But then "coming of age" can be a real plus. A thirty-five-year-old client of mine called in panic. "I'm leaving for a cruise in two weeks. I've spent the last three days covering every store in the city, trying on bathing suits. My choice is between a bathing suit with a fluffy skirt, like my grandmother's, or a soft nonconstructed suit for a twenty-year-old. Where does that leave me?"

If I can tell my age and feel comfortable about it, why should buying clothes make me feel uncomfortable? I could blame it on the manufacturers, since the newest looks are always presented to the public on young, perfectly proportioned bodies. How should women who care about their looks feel about aging? At thirty-five I look in the mirror and think "You look pretty damn good." But I wonder for how long I can enjoy myself in blue jeans and funky clothes. Is there a necessary mode of middle-age dress? I can say yes, reluctantly. It exists, but in varying degrees.

When I see my own hair obviously turning gray, I am realistic enough to know that this means I am over twenty, but I reject the idea that gray hair denotes only aging and unattractiveness. At this time in my life, I am comfortable with my own look as an asset. It is a sophisticated modification of my look. But if your hair, too, is gray, like mine, you will require more color in your make-up to add brightness to your face. You also have the option of coloring the gray. Some other physical changes that appear as we grow older are not so easily dealt with. Skin is less firm, weight is harder to control, and glasses may be necessary. Some people utilize surgical procedures, exercise programs, and "beauty" aids, but anyone doing this should first talk to authorities in each field. Proper foundation and dress choices can be a new alternative to more drastic measures. For example, shorts are comfortable, but they may have been wrong for you even when you were eighteen. If you don't look attractive in shorts, consider cotton culottes, a sundress, wrap skirt, or some new styles in pants.

There are some advantages to reaching a certain age. You become more sure of yourself and this reflects in your clothes. Colors and styles that were too sophisticated now are ideal. If you can spend more money on yourself, you may be able to buy the piece of fine jewelry you have always wanted, or splurge on an expensive pair of shoes.

Just a Little Help

Figure problems that arise with age can be camouflaged. If your neck has become wrinkled, stick to higher necklines or accent with exotic scarves. Several strands of beads will also fill in the neckline. If you want a style that is more revealing, a low back accomplishes this look and is more flattering then a décolleté neckline. If your upper arm isn't firm, a wide array of stoles is available. Tops, dresses, sweaters, and jackets also can cover up, but sometimes short sleeves will be all you need.

If a midriff bulge has appeared, don't wear clinging fabrics or styles that hug your body. Choose an unstructured or soft fabric and style. A more "suited" look is also desirable, either one sold as a suit or one you coordinate yourself with separates. A Chanel style in wool, gabardine, velvet, or linen can be worn during the day with either a shirt or sweater or at night with a satin blouse. A Chanel jacket is loose fitting, and the blouse or sweater can be worn tucked in softly or go over the skirt. Coco Chanel had a wonderful way of conveying through design that age is beautiful.

Feet First

Your legs or thighs may have taken on new shape. Your legs will be revealed most fully in summer clothes. If you live at, or travel to, the beach you will wear a bathing suit much of the time. Concentrate on the area above your waist, and make sure your hair and face are your focal points. If you look good in hats and scarves, wear them.

No one looks at your feet first. Acquire attention just where you want it with chic sunglasses and jewelry pieces that draw attention to your face. Your bathing suit should have color and detail above the waist. And for most thighs, the higher the leg cut of the bathing suit, the more flattering the suit will be. A loose leg ("boy leg" cut) is sometimes slimming too. But don't wear a bathing suit that is cut straight across the leg; this is not a good cut for a thick thigh.

Cover-ups and shawls can become your best friends. Shawls can be tied diagonally across the thigh and hip. No one needs to know that you are doing a bit of hiding. Beachwear can include long skirts, drawstring pants in terrycloth and jersey, beach robes, and jumpsuits. These are all good cover-up modes when you are out of the water and lounging.

Skirt lengths can be a little longer to cover up more of the leg, and hose will give the leg a firmer appearance.

Changing Color

Black seems consistently to be the most controversial color. The argument is either that one is too young to wear black or too old to wear black. Black is beautiful regardless of one's age, but some women are frightened about wearing it. Having worn black since college, I believe that it is the most sophisticated and flattering color I wear, even with my gray hair. Black has no age; I have introduced it frequently with clients over thirty-five. If you have

Cover-ups and shawls can become your best friends. No one needs to know that you are doing a bit of hiding.

not worn black often, it does take time to feel comfortable with it. Try it first combined with another color, or worn only from the waist up. All-black may have to come later. For those who like it, the little black dress with a strand of pearls is always right.

When making wardrobe changes, think of toning down your bright colors. You can stay within the same families of colors, but soften them into dusty tones and pastels. Red can become wine, orange can become apricot, and the neutrals can be combined with darks.

You've got the Cutest Little Baby Face

You say you look cute. Well, why not? Often in my classes this problem is posed, usually by a middle-aged or older woman who has a young face and short stature. Her clothes selection is limited and she is often forced to shop in children's and junior departments because of her size. She feels like a forgotten woman, and often she is. Manufacturers tend to design clothes for the more popular sizes. Choice is narrowed for the small-size woman who wants a more sophisticated look. Style, color, and accessories provide the means of solving the cutesie problem.

Choice is narrowed for the small woman who wants a more sophisticated look. If this is you, stick to the elegant and classic, and avoid a faddish costume look.

When you are looking at styles, stick to the elegant and classic and avoid a faddish costume look, such as a fringed suede skirt and vest. But you aren't stuck with somber tones and dowdy polyester pant suits. Instead, add these looks to your wardrobe: a wool crepe long-sleeved cowl-neck dress worn with a shawl, soft cardigan sweater, or jacket; a gabardine or linen blazer worn with a soft skirt or classic trousers; a long, soft crepe dress with a low V in the back; a velvet dinner suit with a satin shirt; a silk shirtdress (roll up the sleeves and sash the waist); a challis two-piece print skirt and shirt. Some designers have a wonderful approach to making you feel young but not cute. Diane von Furstenberg, Albert Nipon, Jerry Silverman, Liz Claiborne, Jones of New York, and Evan Picone all design with this in mind.

Black and beige are the most sophisticated colors, always chic. Brown, navy blue, gray, burgundy, and white are much better for this purpose than the brights and pastels.

Your accessories should not be cute. Don't use velvet bows, bumblebee earrings, or picnic-basket purses. Choose classic and interesting accessories, not inane ones.

Each stage and age in your life should have positive value for you. In your twenties you can be experimental, in your thirties you want to feel comfortably stable, and past that age you have it made.

3

Your Unique Assets and Figure Problems

How honest and truthful are you with yourself about your body and figure? Are you secure enough to be objective?

Brand-name merchandise is important because you can expect the styles and cuts of certain labels to fit your figure well.

Hips, thighs, and seats are the most difficult areas of the body to camouflage and the most consistent female figure problems.

Letting Some of It Hang Out

Some psychotherapists recommend energetic efforts to express oneself and "let it all hang out." Achieving such a goal is the result of practice and discipline, though the result is expected to appear spontaneous and natural. The poet Yeats tells us, "we must labor to be beautiful." Since our culture values the slender body, you learn to work at being thin in order to look better in whatever you wear. Certain shapes and lines of the body (nose, ear, mouth, hands) are considered attractive; no one has all the right lines, however.

Keeping your body in shape and limiting your food intake require effort every day of your life. However, some aims may seem impossible because of your inheritance. I remember vividly that my grandmother was stunning, always elegantly dressed, but that she had shapeless legs. The legs were my inheritance, and for years I daydreamed of having Betty Grable legs. After participating in every available exercise course, experimenting with innumerable gimmicks (rubbing my legs with creams, cellulite sponges, and vibrators), playing hours of tennis, and jogging until I hated it, I have finally accepted my own legs. This has now allowed me to approach my leg problem as a fashion problem, to use principles of camouflage, and to accentuate the positive and draw attention away from the negative.

Self-analysis

How honest and truthful are you with yourself about your body and figure? Are you secure enough to be objective? In order to do the best with what you've got, take the time to think about your figure. Do this alone, without help from anyone else. What do you like and dislike about your figure? If you can't think of any positives you are probably in a depressed mood and should postpone this evaluation. Your attitude toward yourself will probably be less critical when you realize that there are no perfect bodies or figures. The chances are that your own figure is better than average in several ways.

It may also help you psychologically to realize that what we like or dislike about our bodies is not the result of some absolute standard, but only a cultural and relative assumption. There is nothing biologically wrong with big ears, for example.

What's Yours Is Yours, What's Hers Is Hers

Learning what to do with what you've got will be more possible if you first accept various realities. Don't generalize about having a "good" figure or a "bad" figure. It is much more meaningful and helpful to arrive at specific conclusions: "My legs are only 25 percent of perfection," or "My hair is about 90 percent perfect." It is sometimes comforting, too, to remember that you have a heart, brain, a family, a job, a sense of values, and that all these things can be included in your total self-evaluation.

If Fitting Rooms Were Bugged

A hidden microphone in a fitting room would pick up such muted phrases as, "It will never fit," "My diet begins Monday," "After all, I've had two

How honest are you about your figure? Use these principles to camouflage: dark colors, solids, no patterns.

children" (that was seven years ago), "Surely these pants are mismarked, I know I wear a size ten," "I haven't eaten a thing all day." Working with women in fitting rooms for years I've learned to tune into these problems of attitude and information. Few women accept their imperfect figures (attitude problem), and fewer still realize they can take off five apparent pounds and a few inches from their frames by choosing the right clothes for their figures (information problem). Attitude problems are widespread and cause much harm. One of my purposes throughout this book is to help readers identify their self-defeating tendencies (such as generalizing about their figures being "good" or "bad," or constantly wishing that their inherited features were different.)

Brand Names Do Make a Figure Difference

Brands are very important because of individual brand styles and cuts. When you find a particular brand that is flattering to your figure, keep the tag from the garment and write down on it the name of the store where you bought it. Though styles do vary, the basic patterns of cut often remain similar for the same brand. For example, Anne Klein has a full pant leg, Act III is cut full all over, and Butte Knit cuts for the more mature figure. If a garment fits you especially well, consider buying the garment in two different colors or patterns. I have trouble finding pants that are comfortable and well-fitting . I have narrowed down my selections to two or three brands and I always buy the same ones, limiting my colors to no more than three in my entire wardrobe. I know the stores where I can find them, and in this way I have simplified what was once a difficult and frustrating problem. I always feel comfortable and I look thinner too. (My own special delusion is that I could never be too thin.)

Put Your Money Where Your Weight Is

Since some brands are more expensive than others, your rule should be to put your money where your figure needs the most assistance. Watch for sales of your favorite items. If you have difficulty in buying tops that are flattering, and certain better brands look good on you, buy the better ones and spend less for what goes on the bottom. If the color is one you wear very often, buy two exactly alike. This will prevent the one garment from wearing out and will assure you that one will always be clean and ready for wearing. Remember that an expensive purchase should be considered an investment for a special reason.

Choosing to Look Taller

If you are short you are very conscious that the higher your heel the taller you will look. But be careful not to choose a heel height that will make you awkward and uncertain about your movements. A heel that is too high can cause the body to look unbalanced.

An outfit of unified or single color adds apparent length to the body. When you use more than one color, especially contrasting ones, the body seems "cut" and therefore shorter. This "cut" effect will also happen with patterns, unless they are small and run vertically. You are generally better off with monotones, except for accessories, if you wish to appear taller. Use color or contrast near the face to keep the focus up. For example, a black cowl-neck sweater with gold and silver chains at the neckline; or a dress of navy blue linen trimmed with white piqué. Jewelry, scarves, and detail will help achieve this.

Avoid most belts unless you are thin, since these too will make your figure appear divided. A narrow belt of the same color as the garment is best, and do not tie it too tightly.

Beware of high-fashion styles that would make you look shorter, and of fabrics that are heavy and would appear to weigh you down. Be very careful of capes, dolman sleeves, drop shoulders, very full sleeves, turtlenecks that are too high under the chin, and tops and bottoms that billow and lose you. Some other poor choices for short people are high waists (unless you are thin), jackets that are too long, and very full skirts or pants.

Hemlines are important; a length approximately 2 or 3 inches below the knee should be the most comfortable and look best. Yes, if you are short you can wear boots. Be sure the heel is at least 3 inches high and that the hem of your skirt goes over the boot top, otherwise you will have flesh or a constrasting stocking fabric showing. When this happens, the eye will move downward, breaking the overall appearance of length. If your hemline is slightly shorter than this (a length from a previous season), match the stocking color as closely as possible to the boot and the hemline color to avoid a distraction.

Choose fabrics cautiously; stay away from bold patterns, bulky knits, wide-wale corduroy, quilted fabrics, meltons, heavy wools and garments that are too heavily lined. Your preferences should be for silks, challis, soft wools and cashmere, cottons, linens and other fabrics that are soft and light.

Accessories should be in proportion for short people. If you wear a shoulder bag, it should not be heavy, large or give you a droopy appearance. The shape of the bag should not be bulky.

Clunky, oversized jewelry also is taboo when you are short, unless you wear one large, simple piece along with lighter ones. Otherwise your jewelry will be ostentatious rather than enhancing what you are wearing. What you

To give a taller appearance, stick to soft, simple styling. No vivid prints. What you wear around your neck and on your ears should not be heavy.

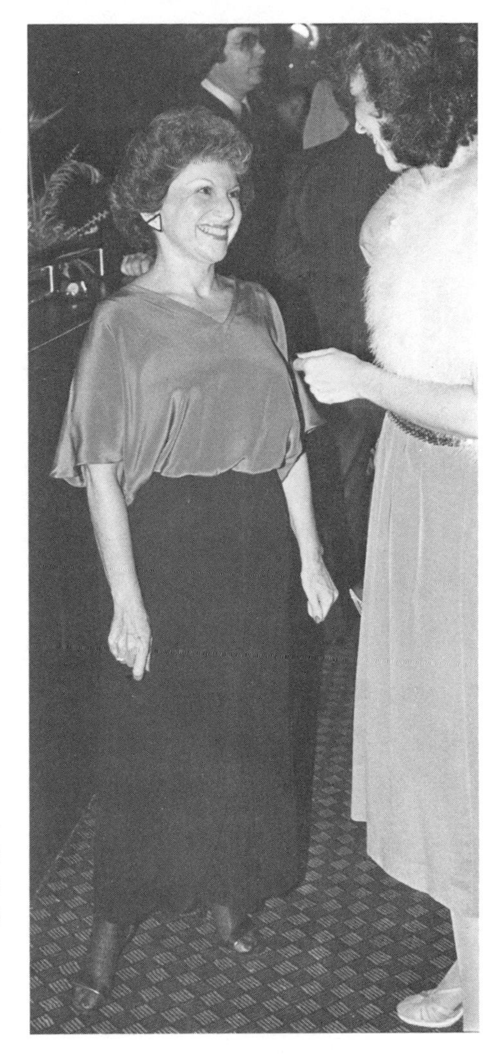

If you are short and wish to appear taller, stick to simple styles and lightweight fabrics. This correct hem length also gives the illusion of height.

wear around your neck and on your ears should be light, since you do not want to give a weighted-down appearance at the neckline or around your face. For an interesting effect, when you choose pins, make them not too large but add more than one. For example, a pair, or two that are different, may be placed on your shoulder in a direction moving away from your body for a sweeping effect.

If you are buying a fur, the pelts should be smooth, flat, or sheared, and in many cases a single-breasted style will be superior. The key to looking taller is to wear clothes that do not compete with your size and that draw the eye in an upward movement.

Hemlines are important. When you wear boots, be sure the skirt hem goes over the boot top. With flesh showing, the eye is drawn downward, breaking the all-over appearance.

Being Tall

If you are tall, you almost always have an advantage when selecting clothes because of the general nature of fashions. However, there are times when you must be cautious in your selections. Heel heights can be as high as you are comfortable with. If you are thin, a very narrow heel is fine. But if you are heavier, the heel should be less tapered, so that you won't look top heavy. A very low heel or a flat shoe will seem unbalanced unless your figure and legs are thin. If they are not, stay away from heels lower than 2 inches, unless you are choosing a shoe for comfort only (walking, touring, athletics).

You can be flexible with color. Color near the face adds length. Enjoy one color or several. If your waist is long and narrow, wear interesting belts of any width; make the belt an important point of your entire silhouette.

Enjoy playing with fabrics if you are tall. You may select almost any, from lightweight to heavy, but always remember that the heavier the fabric, the heavier you will look. If you want to use a bulky fabric, consider choosing it for one area of your body (the slimmest) and combining it with lighter weights rather than using it all over. Avoid layering bulky weights; no matter how thin you are, no body needs that much extra padding. Wide-wale corduroy, quilted fabrics, bulky knits, mohairs, meltons, and wool tweeds can be worn more easily by those who are taller and thinner.

Large, bold patterns will make you look wider, not taller, and bright colors call attention, so be careful to put them only where you want them to be noticed.

Tall persons have wider styling choices; they can wear high necklines, fuller shoulders and sleeves, longer jackets, fuller skirts and pants, and more variable skirt lengths.

Accentuating the Specifics

THE NECKLINE

To appear broader or longer

Open, flat collars
Plunging necklines
Ruffles, tiers
Heavy jewelry
Long necklaces
Bright colors and vivid patterns

These will make the neckline appear longer and more open, but if your neck is very short be careful to select only flat open collars and a plunging neckline.

To appear shorter

Turtle necks
Cowl necks
High collars
Wide necklaces
Ascots

Most of the time a long neck is very positive. However, if you want your neck to appear shorter, styling is important.

SHOULDERS

To appear broader

Padded shoulders, drop shoulders, epaulets, dolman sleeves
Unconstructed jacket, fullness beginning at the shoulder in blouses, sweaters, and jackets
Bulky fabrics
Large or busy patterns
Shoulder detail — pleats, contrasting stitching, trims, braids, and buttons
Pockets

To appear narrower

Tapered jackets, sweaters, and blouses
Smooth fabrics
Dark solid colors
Little or no trim, simple detail
Narrow sleeves
Set-in sleeves

BUSTLINE

To appear fuller

Bright colors, light colors, and contrasted coloring
Patterns
Bust pockets
Seams, tucks, gathers, shearing, ruffles, bust darts, contrasted stitching, trims

Bulky, heavy, clingy, ribbed, or textured fabrics
Layered clothing, a vest with detail and color
Heavy jewelry
Chains, beads, scarves, or pins placed or hanging on or near the bosom

To appear smaller

No patterns, trims, tucks, gathers, dart stitching, or pockets on the bosom
Dark, solid colors
Smooth, flat fabrics
Very little layering except for lightweight fabrics of the same color
A vest in dark color, worn unbuttoned
Soft or loose-hanging clothes
No jewelry or scarves on the bosom; chains and necklaces should not be heavy or large or hang on the bosom, but be placed at the neckline or well below the bosom
Waistlines should not be high, which emphasizes the bustline

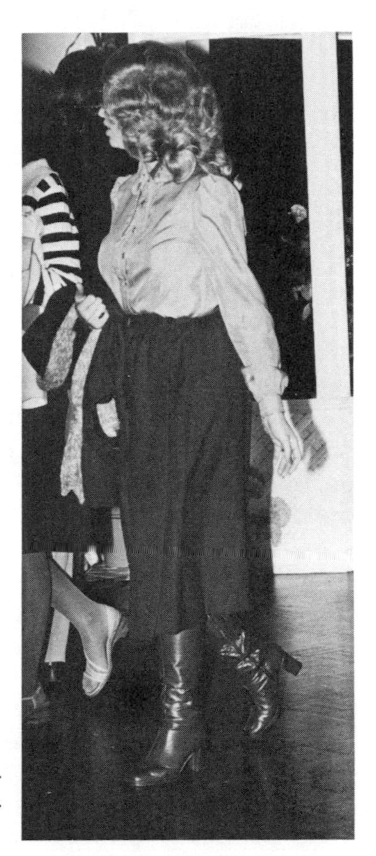

If your bustline is not one of your best features, de-emphasize it by wearing dark colors on top and loose-hanging clothes.

You may not consider your bustline one of your best features. In this case, call little attention to the area by wearing dark solid colors and placing your jewelry or scarves at the neck or on the shoulders. Wear designs that are uncluttered and simply cut.

THE WAISTLINE

To appear longer

A narrow belt at the waist or over a top that is allowed to hang on the outside
Matching belts
One color on the silhouette
Low waistlines

Tops can be worn in or out, providing they are not of a heavy fabric. If your waist is narrow, tuck your tops inside.

To appear shorter-waisted

Wide belts
High-waisted pants and/or skirts
Contrasting colors meeting at the waistline

To appear narrower

Dark colors
Smooth textures
Belts (only if your waistline is already narrow)

If your waistline is thick, and you do not want to call attention to it, choose a tunic or wear your top on the outside hanging softly below the waist; do not wear a blouson-style top. Use solid, dark colors without pockets, belts, or added accents at the waistline. However, if your waist is small and you want it to be a focal point, wear your top on the inside, fitted close to the body, and do wear a decorative belt or accentuate the area with pockets, buttons, trim, or contrasting colors. When wearing your top inside, be careful not to choose a heavy, bulky fabric that will add unnecessary thickness.

Remember that pockets, trims, and any other waistline detail will move the eye to that point; add these only if you want attention there. Otherwise, buy pants and skirts that are basic, or remove the details yourself. Usually this will not detract from the style of the garment. Unless you feel the pockets are functional, and in most cases they are not, always have them removed to avoid unnecessary attention to the waist. This is especially important if you

For a slimmer waistline and middle, wear solid colors, not prints. A top, vest, or jacket worn on the outside will make you appear narrower.

can see the pocket or lining through the pant or skirt (which occurs often with white). Never fill the pockets, since they will appear bulky. (Most men's tight-fitting French pants have no pockets, except for a tiny coin pocket.)

Elastic waistbands can help for a smooth waistline, but be sure the elastic is not too wide or too thick, especially if you are short-waisted.

THE ABDOMEN

To appear flatter

Slimming undergarments (see below)
Dark colors over the stomach
Solids; no prints, stripes, or patterns
Smooth fabrics
Pleats only if they are few and very narrow
No belts, ties, or sashes on the stomach

For a flatter tummy, begin with your undergarment. Be careful to find a salesperson who is knowledgeable about today's undergarments, including pantyhose. She must be able to advise you on proper fit. To save money, select a nude tone, which will work well under all colors and especially under white, since white undergarments worn under white clothes almost always show through. Do not choose trimmed or lace undergarments since you are looking for the smoothest effect possible. Pantyhose and support pantyhose (always buy the "control top" type) are today's best buy on the market for a natural, comfortable, and smooth result. They produce a flatter look from the waist through the hip area. No matter how thin you are, you want whatever weight is there to appear smooth and not flabby. If you need more support than this, try a lightweight control panty brief worn in addition to your panty hose (see Chapter 5 for more undergarment specifics).

Tops can be tucked inside, blouse them *softly,* but do not select a blouson, which will call attention to the stomach. If your stomach is very noticeable, wear your top on the outside, but be extremely cautious not to choose a top or jacket that ends at the stomach; it must fall below the area, preferably below the hips. Also, take care in the fit. A jacket should never be too tight and usually it is better worn unbuttoned so that it doesn't pull over the area. Adhere to the same rules when selecting a sweater to be worn as a jacket, and never select a bulky or clingy knit. If the jacket has a belt, tie it loosely or remove it. Belt loops usually are unnecessary too.

HIPS, THIGHS, AND SEAT

Let me be the first to congratulate you if this is a positive area of your figure. For myself included, this seems to be the most difficult area to camou-

To make your hips, thighs, and seat appear smaller, clothes should be in solid colors. Tops and jackets should come to the waist or well below the seat. Do not contrast colors in this area. See the following page for flattering combinations.

flage and the most consistent female figure problem. You will have to take time and experiment with many different brands to find the garment that offers you the best fit. When you find a flattering and comfortable brand, stick with it.

To make smaller

Side-zipped pants and skirts
Dark colors, never white or pastels
No color contrasts
No patterns
Tops, vests, jackets, and sweaters ending either at the waist or below the seat, never at the thigh
No drop waists or low torsos
Skirts and dresses with a soft flow and minimum fullness
No sashes, belts, buttons, or ties
Pockets *only* if very unobtrusive

Always, always, always look at yourself from the front and from the back in a mirror. If you have a three-way mirror you will be able to see all angles properly. Many women, I'm sure, never get a rear view of themselves; if they did they would surely dead-bolt their refrigerators. Notice the rear view of others the next time you're in a grocery store, hotel, or airport.

The coat in the center is flattering to the figure. The two jackets and plaid skirts are unattractive on the figures. The skirts should be solid and longer, worn with coats covering the hemline.

LEGS

To appear fuller

This may be difficult to achieve, but begin with a pant or skirt style that has fullness beginning at the top of the thigh, such as a pajama style which hangs soft, loose, and away from the body. This will improve skinny legs; your skirt or dress can be full, pleated, or dirndl style; and a longer length, if you are not too short, will be most attractive.

For the bottom, choose patterns, stripes, or plaids. Colors may vary, but lights and brights will give a fuller appearance.

Pockets, trims, appliqués, and anything decorative will add fullness but will also call attention to the area, so unless you want the eye to focus there, a plainer look may be a necessary compromise.

Colored or textured stockings call attention to the leg and gives it a bolder and less skinny look. (This is the opposite of wearing black, gray, or textured stockings for a slimmer appearance, which is a common but false idea.)

Avoid wearing very high or pointed heels. Use lower heels.

Clothes that are layered over the entire silhouette add fullness (but can also hide overweight bulges, provided the fabric is not clingy).

If your legs are shapely and are a positive physical attribute, use some of the above suggestions to call attention to them. Decorative hems, hose, and shoes all will be eyecatchers.

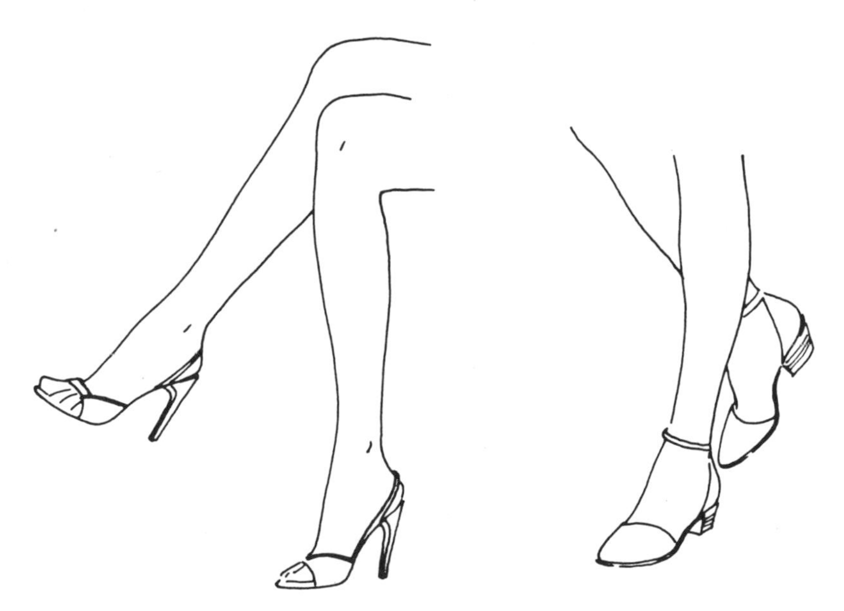

The higher the heel the slimmer the leg will appear.

To appear slimmer

Darker colors and simpler styles will call less attention to legs. Your skirt and pant choices should be soft and not clingy. They can be straight or slightly full, but never knit.

Wear natural or nude hose (no pattern or texture).

The higher the heel of your shoe the slimmer the leg will appear. Hem lengths must vary according to your height and the heel height. Plain hemlines (no flounces, beads, scallops, etc.) are best.

THE FEET

To appear smaller, shorter

If your feet seem always to get in your way as attention-getters, when ideally you would like them to disappear, wear a plain-styled, neutral-colored shoe. Never white, unless you are wearing white pants, since a white shoe is certain to attract attention. Bone or beige will be the least conspicuous. If your clothing is dark, wear navy blue, brown, or black shoes with a neutral stocking or knee-high sock. Or choose an opaque stocking and a matching shoe color. If what you are wearing is light or pastel, a bone or beige shoe is best worn with a neutral stocking. The basic principle is that color differentiation focuses attention. Avoid dyed-to-match or multicolored shoes.

The best styles for this problem are a simple pump, a sandal void of detail, or a classic boot. If your shoe has an open toe, do not use a colored toe nail polish, since it will draw attention.

When wearing a long skirt or dress, either formal or informal, wear shoes of a neutral color — avoid silver, gold, or fancy detail. Try to match your hem color to the shoe. Select a satin, suede, or leather shoe fabric rather than something novel.

To appear longer

Only if your feet are unusually small would you want to make them appear larger. Be certain, if you are trying to add length to your feet, that you are achieving this aim and not simply drawing attention to your feet. An open toe and heel add length to the foot. White and colored shoes appear longer too. It is usually better to treat your feet as a portion of the whole body, rather than as a particular, and to stick to basic styles and colors to reduce mistakes in coordinating.

Making Your Components Work Together

Your bodily presentation should reflect a complete interpretation, highlighting your assets and minimizing your negatives. When you have made an honest evaluation of yourself physically and have spent time experimenting, you will achieve a more attractive presentation of your figure.

Remember, also, that change is a constant feature of life. Your body will change, and the retail market will offer new brands, new styles, and new products to work with.

The Clothes

4

Closet Organization and Clothes Care

If you value your appearance, also value your closet — as a means to an end.

The clothes you wear most often should hang at the easiest-to-reach places in the closet.

Keep your cleaning bills to a minimum. Most people overclean their clothes.

In college, I was sometimes closeted with my clothes more than with my books. One day I came back to my dorm room to find that three of my closest chums had delightedly unorganized my overorganized closet. I was told that no one at college should take pride in her closet. But *I* did and I do value such neatness and organization, despite the time and energy it requires. Some persons or families have not learned such organization or they choose not to do it; some even seem to resent it. If you value your appearance, also value your closet — as a means to an end.

Very, Very Small Rooms

What makes a closet functional? No matter how limited your space, hang your clothes systematically. Otherwise some clothes will go unnoticed and probably unworn because they are misplaced. Think about it like this: a closet is a small room in which you spend significant time. It can also be a decorative room. Even though the space may be limited, use it as a hideaway or enjoy it as a quiet place of your own.

To make a small space appear larger, mirror the walls. For decorative purposes and easy maintenance, use wallpaper that has a vinyl or wipe-off surface. Add carpeting or rugs and shelf-paper trim for a finished look. And if space is not so limited, anything goes. Try plants, a lounge chair, a step stool to reach shelves, or stereo music piped in. Your closet should be pretty, and it can be fun.

Closet Interior Design

Consider the following basic plan: a single hanging rod across one side, and another single rod or two rods on the opposite wall. If you are working with a small or shallow space, use two-thirds of your space for single hanging (long garments) and one-third for double hanging (separates). Shoes do best on deep shelves in boxes. If space is very limited, use a hanging fabric shoe caddy (holds about twelve pair) or a metal rack (holds about eighteen pair) that can be wall-mounted or hung on the inside of the door. A floor shoe rack, available in different sizes, always can be used for extras and for the shoes you wear most often. Put handbags on narrow shelves. There are decorative quilted closet bags for this purpose if you do not have shelf or drawer space.

A full-length mirror should be in the closet, on the closet door, or very nearby. A three-way full-length mirror is best if space allows. Good lighting is critical, and unfortunately most closets are quite dim. More than one light is needed for adequate lighting, and if you are designing your closet, a skylight in the ceiling, with additional electric lighting is ideal. When possible, your light switch should be on the outside of the closet, for easy lighting before entering. A battery-operated extra light can be mounted in your closet at a very low cost.

Presto, It's a Closet

It may be that there are no closets where you are living, or that you need additional closet space. An armoire (large wardrobe or cabinet) can be both decorative and functional in your room. If you scout around antique shops you can discover them, some costly, some more reasonably priced. There are many styles, so select the one that is most serviceable for you. Does the armoire have drawer space, is there a mirror, is it deep enough? Are the shelves and doors sturdy? You will find armoires that are brand new, perhaps even of unfinished wood, in stores or in catalogues. Enjoy decorating them. The shelves and drawers can be lined and lights installed; most of them can be locked. For other armoire-decorating ideas, browse through antiques and home decorating magazines.

Equipment for the Closet

Hangers can be matching and decorative, and should be either plastic, fabric, or quilted. Be sure you have some quilted ones for knits and other garments that pull out of shape easily and for those that tend to slide off plastic hangers.

Skirt hangers, usually metal or wood, are used for skirts and pants. Be sure the edges of the hanger clips are smooth to avoid pressure marks on the garments. An additional precaution in hanging fabrics that easily mark, such as velvet, suede, and corduroy, is to put tissue paper at the points where the fabric is clipped. There are two-way hangers for hanging a top and a bottom on one hanger. These save space in your closet.

Rod covers are made of colored plastic and fit over closet rods to permit easy sliding of hangers and to cover unattractive closet rods. These covers can be cut to fit the length of the rod, and two can be fitted together end to end for longer rods. (They are pretty over shower rods, too.) Rod covers are inexpensive and can be purchased at many bath shops or department store bath departments.

Shoe boxes are best if made of clear plastic with slide-out drawers for easy access. Lift-off lids are harder to use. The box the shoes came in also can be used and can be covered with attractive fabric or paper and labeled on the outside, since memory is not perfect.

Purse covers and boxes of clear plastic work well. Do not use such covers for patent leather, however, unless you first wrap the purse in tissue, since plastic sometimes sticks.

Belt racks are easiest to use when long and narrow with individual hooks. I do not recommend the round belt hanger, since it does not allow easy access to an individual belt. Belt racks may be used also for jewelry chains. Usually they are mounted on the wall inside the closet. Use two, if necessary.

Closet hooks are available in decorative clear or colored plastic or porcelain. Use sturdy ones and have them mounted securely on the back of the closet door or within the closet. Use them for robes, nightgowns, or clothes you might wear again that day.

More closet accessories which should always be on hand, in or near your closet, include —

Shoe brush
Shoe horn

Clothes brush
Sachet
Scotch tape for lint removal
Cloths for wiping shoe heels, soles, and handbags
Spot removers, dry and liquid
Closet freshener and moth crystals
Shoe mittens
Hand clothes steamer

Choose one spot remover of each type. Before using, always experiment on the inside of the garment in an inconspicuous place, such as the inside of the hemline, and then use on the inside of the spot first. Chemistry is complex and not always predictable.

Moth cakes are preferable to the crystals, since the odor of crystals is too strong unless you are storing out-of-season clothes. When you use the freshener and cakes, be sure they are in plastic closet cases with small holes; this reduces odor and prevents spillage.

Shoes that are exposed in the closet and not worn often should be put in shoe mittens.

A hand clothes steamer is a wonderful item for home and travel. You steam wrinkles out instead of pressing them. It is small and easy to use on men's and women's clothes and saves time and money. A steamer can be bought in hardware stores and notions departments for under $16. I use mine daily and never travel without it.

The Art of Hanging

Hangers should always face in the same direction. That way they look neater, move more easily, and take up less space. The clothes you wear most often should hang at the easiest-to-reach places in the closet.

Hang clothes together by categories:

Pants
Skirts
Dresses
Pantsuits
Active sportswear (tennis, golf, etc.)
Evening clothes
Sleepwear (robes and gowns)
Outerwear (jackets, coats, raincoats)

If you are using double hanging rods, put pants and skirts on the bottom, and blouses, sweaters, and other tops on the upper rod. This separates the categories in the closet, gives a neater appearance, and permits you to visually coordinate tops and bottoms. Because of the longer pant styles today, some pants may drag on the floor. If this occurs, double the pants over a hanger but be sure to put tissue in the folds to prevent wrinkles.

Out-of-Season Clothes

If you are using the same closet for out-of-season clothes, keep them at the back of the closet in plastic or fabric garment bags. Your closet should be kept at a cool temperature. Lower the heat when you are away from the house, and open the closet door often to permit ventilation, especially for furs. If you can use a separate closet for storing winter clothes, sprinkle moth crystals on the bottom of the closet and on shelves twice during the warm months. A moth spray is also good, but be sure not to spray the clothes directly. Keep your clothes covered or in garment bags to keep them free of dust.

Healthy Closet Compulsions

Return your clothes to the closet only when they are ready to wear. This means that the clothes are dry, pressed (if necessary), checked for missing buttons and loose threads, and by all means clean.

Reorganize your closet at least twice a year by ridding it of any clothes or accessories that you have not worn in the last two years. If you have not worn them in that length of time, you never will. Donate such clothes to charity, sell them, or send them to a consignment shop and use any money you get for new purchases. But do not keep in your closet any clothes you are not wearing. They will only take up space and cause a well-organized closet to become cluttered. Once they are out of the closet, you won't miss them or feel guilty about not wearing them. This technique will become easier each season, and you will be wearing only what you feel good in.

Keep clothes that are fragile (lace, beads, suede, velvet) in garment bags to assure proper protection.

Don't hang furs (fun furs or real ones) in plastic bags, unless these bags have been properly treated for using with fur. Costly furs should be put in professional fur storage for the spring and summer months.

Don't hang furs, suedes, or mohairs next to fabrics on which they may shed, such as velvet, wool, or corduroy.

Don't put any clothes or shoes back into the closet after wearing them unless they have been aired outside the closet for at least two hours. Your clothes will stay fresher and will unwrinkle faster if you adhere to this rule.

Don't put damp clothes, especially rainwear or shoes that have wet soles, into the closet until they are completely dry. This may take overnight.

To Clean or Not to Clean

Keep your cleaning bills to a minimum. Most people overclean their clothes. Washing and cleaning are very hard on fabrics. It is usually not necessary to wash or clean your clothes after every wearing. Each time you put something through this process you are taking a chance: regardless of how costly a garment is, most fabrics are susceptible to shrinkage, fading, loss of body and shape. If the slacks you first wore last week were the right length then, and now, after cleaning, are too short, you can be sure you did not grow taller or wider. If you are using a custom cleaner, ask them to do the cleaning by hand, and to measure the garments before and after; ask them not to press creases or hems. Request that hems and collars be hand rolled. This will prevent fabrics from becoming shiny, and if the garments need altering at a later date, the cleaning creases will not be so hard to remove.

If you are washing your clothes, do it by hand and don't dry them in a dryer. If the garment is new, have it dry cleaned the first few times, then wash. Even jeans will stay a better color and shape if they are cleaned in the beginning. Many people always dry clean their jeans. Cleaning and washing also may damage buttons. Have decorative buttons (suede, stones, velvet, etc.) removed by the cleaner before the garment is cleaned. If you are good at spot cleaning, do this to avoid allover cleaning or washing. If you know what spotted the garment (perfume, water, gravy), you will get more effective cleaning.

Helpful Hints

Use pant or skirt hangers to prevent creases in slacks; do not fold slacks over a standard wire hanger

Sweaters should be dried flat, on a towel.

Blouses, jackets, dresses, skirts, and most tops should be dried on a nonmetal hanger, since wire causes rust stains. Drying on a hanger will shape the garment while it is wet.

To avoid fading, most dark colors should be washed alone, in cool water.

Know the strength of bleach and spot cleaners and control the amount you use by applying it only to the specific area with a white cloth or cotton ball.

Be sure to remove any jewelry from the garment before washing or cleaning.

Pressing

Never begin with a hot iron. Before you put the iron on the garment, test it on a cloth or with your hand. Most irons are easy to regulate. On many fabrics you must be extremely cautious about temperature. These include silk, Quiana, acetate, polyester, crepe, voile, and satin. Almost all garments should be pressed on the "wrong" side to prevent streaks, shines, and iron marks. This is especially true when the color is dark and the fabric is crepe, satin, velvet or corduroy. My best advice is to use your clothes' best friend, a hand steamer.

Your Body and Your Clothes

If you can get into the habit of taking off your clothes and airing them out immediately, you will keep them in better condition. Before you return them to your closet, hang them on a rack or over a door or any place they are not enclosed. Leave them out for several hours. Wrinkles and odor will be much less or will even disappear. In your closet, try to hang them at least a half-inch apart. Never cram garments against one another.

If you perspire a lot, use underarm shields and never put perfume directly on your clothes.

After you have used cream or lotion on your skin, wait until it has been absorbed before you dress.

The Care and Storing of Accessories

Accessories include jewelry, scarves, belts, lingerie, hosiery, socks, and purses. If your accessories are properly organized, you will enjoy using them.

Drawers. Whether you are using a piece of furniture or a built-in space, drawers are the most important feature to consider. You will need deep and shallow drawers, and small drawers. Line drawers with fabric or paper. If you use paper, choose one with a wipeable surface and an adhesive backing. Fabric should be fitted in the drawer, but left loose so it can be removed for cleaning. Some lining paper is perfumed; otherwise you can put a sachet in with your underwear and lingerie. If you have a used bottle of a favorite perfume, put the empty bottle (uncapped) in the drawer; the fragrance will last for weeks.

Jewelry Drawer. If you are using a jewelry drawer, chest or individual box, it should be lined with a soft fabric, such as velvet, satin, or Pacific cloth. This keeps jewelry from getting scratched and from moving when the drawer is opened and closed. The best drawers for jewelry are small and divided. You can buy dividers or use small containers that will fit into the drawer. If you are using a chest, one with individual drawers will be best for keeping your jewelry organized. Arrange the pieces by categories: chains, pins, earrings, etc. Any pieces that are very costly or of sentimental value should be kept in a bank vault. Keep polishing cloths in the drawer, one for gold, one for silver. Always keep your jewelry shiny. Some pieces, such as earrings and necklaces, may be hung up for easy access. Special stands are made for holding necklaces and earrings. These are especially convenient for pieces you wear often. Keep a dish nearby on which to place your jewelry as you remove it, or place pieces immediately back in their drawer.

Scarves. If you keep scarves in a drawer, put the ones you wear most often on top. If they wrinkle easily, put tissue between the folds. Larger ones can be hung on smooth hooks, or folded over a hanger. Be certain to check them after each wearing to see if they are spotted with make-up or perfume.

Belts. Hang belts or fold them in drawers. If they are decorative and contain stones or metal buckles, they should be wrapped in tissue to prevent scratching. Those that might tarnish can be wrapped in Pacific cloth.

Purses. If you have the space for it, keep purses in drawers. Any that can be easily scratched (suede, patent leather, smooth leather) should be wrapped in tissue or cloth. If the purse or its handle has any kind of metal or chain, do not let it rest on the purse, as it often marks the surface. A purse that can easily lose its shape should be stored with tissue paper inside. Never leave mints, gum, or other foods in the purse.

Lingerie, Underwear. One large divided drawer or separate drawers will be needed for your underwear. Separate them into categories: bras, slips, panties, etc. Always keep on top what you wear most often. You may also want to separate them by color. If you wear separate underwear for sports (tennis pants, socks), arrange these together. Slips should be kept by style and length. Keep a sachet in these drawers. Socks and hosiery should be paired and kept by style (sandal-foot, reinforced toe) and color. They should be kept on a soft surface or in individual bags. Hosiery boxes can be bought in quilted fabrics.

Sleepwear. Hang or fold your sleepwear. Long robes and nightgowns will take up less space hanging, and will wrinkle much less. If you have a fragile gown or robe that you do not wear often (your honeymoon treasure, perhaps) , keep it in a separate garment bag. Use sachet around the hangers and in the drawer.

Foldables. Sweaters and knits usually hold their shape better if they are laid folded in drawers. For this you can buy individual bags that either zip or fold closed. Use these bags for gloves and mittens also. Tissue between the folds will help prevent wrinkles.

Storing Accessories. If you are storing out-of-season accessories, be sure you put them away clean and repaired. If they are wool, put a moth cake in the drawer.

And Now for the Challenge

Do you dare take a look at your closet? When you do, does everything in it come tumbling down? If the answer is "yes," I suggest you reread this chapter as a first step in getting your closet organized.

5

The Fit Makes the Difference

Before you make a decision on fit, look at yourself in a full-length, three-way mirror.

The garments you wear underneath your clothes will significantly affect your appearance.

Have your undergarments properly fitted.

Regardless of how much you like a garment, it has to fit well or it will be uncomfortable and look unbecoming on you. Feeling good in what you wear is as important as looking good. Before you make a decision on a garment, look at yourself in a full-length three-way mirror so you can see yourself from all angles. Sit, bend, and stretch. Can you move easily? Is the garment roomy but not baggy? Is it the best possible look for your figure? Should you try a smaller or a larger size? Size, remember, is relative. Sweaters are sized differently from blouses; pants differently from pantsuits; dresses, coats, and suits by still another method. In addition, sizes are cut differently depending on the designer. Alterations frequently are necessary to make garments fit you. If you do not wear the same size top and bottom, you should buy coordinated separates instead of buying one-piece garments.

What You Should Know About Alterations

All styles and fabrics respond differently to alteration so be sure you select a knowledgeable fitter. If you do your own alterations you should be

Are your pants roomy enough? Can you move comfortably and attractively in your clothes? These pants fit these women well.

fully informed before you begin. Know first the fabric content in order to know how the fabric will respond to alterations. Can it be altered without leaving permanent lines and creases? Many durable-press fabrics show pressing marks. Has the fabric been "preshrunk"? Some fabrics shrink when cleaned or laundered: cotton, denim, crepe, some polyesters. Some stretch: knits, loose weaves, matte jersey. For good tailoring you should know these facts. When buying clothes, consider the extra cost of alterations, since you may decide not to buy something that requires expensive adjustments. If extensive alterations are required, chances are the garment will never fit satisfactorily.

Examine the way a garment is cut, put together, and finished. Alterations often require generous fabric allowance for seams, hems, pleats, and sleeve lengths. If the fabric is patterned, striped, checked or plaid, look at the seams of the entire garment to be sure you won't have trouble making the design match during alterations.

Here are some additional ideas you may want to consider at the time you make a purchase or have a garment altered.

- On most garments belt loops are unnecessary and unattractive, especially if they are string loops; if this is the case, have them removed.

- Remove labels, especially those on accessories (scarves, gloves, etc.); they show when you don't want them to and usually they come unstitched or ravel. Keep the labels if they include information you will need at a later time. Be sure to write on the label what garment it came from.

- If the buttons on a garment are covered with the same fabric or are decorative, an extra one may be sewn into the inside of the garment. If not, ask the store at the time of purchase to order an extra one for you. There is usually a charge for this service, but it can save you even more money in the long run if you should lose a button.

- If the store is making your alterations, ask that all buttons and snaps be checked to be sure they are secure.

The Big Pants-Length Problem

Have you ever found yourself just looking at people? The next time make it more interesting by looking at the fit of their clothes. Start at the feet, since the most common error is in the pants length. Whether worn by men or

Pant lengths should never be too short. This is an appropriate length.

women, nine out of ten times the pants will be ridiculously short, and the tenth time they will be too long. A pair of pants should be hemmed to hang approximately one-half inch from the floor. Alterations should allow for shrinkage after the first cleaning or washing. Because you will wear different heel heights with your pants, be sure alterations are made with the shoe you will wear. Otherwise new pants can look like last year's that shrank two sizes. If you buy a pair of "high fashion" pants, the style for the season may be tapered and very short, to be worn with a slim high-heeled shoe, or baggy and very short. These pants would be shorter than most others you have in your wardrobe.

Regardless of what hem you are shortening (skirt, dress, pants, jacket), do not cut off all the fabric, or leave so much that the hem is bulky. A hem gives a finished look and allows for letting out at a later time. Some of the newer skirts and dresses are finished with no hem, so be careful when shortening these to be as exact as possible.

Zippers, Buttons, and Linings

Zippers and other closures can detract from the garment if they are not put in properly. Be sure they close securely, that the color does not contrast with the garment, that it is sewn flat into the garment and does not pull or gape. Closures should open and close easily and allow enough room for getting in and out of the garment.

Be sure the buttons are sized correctly for the button holes. I have had blouses on which the button holes frayed or stretched after several wearings and the blouse would not stay buttoned. Button holes that are bound securely usually will prevent this from happening.

A lining adds a finished look to clothes and gives body to the garment. Not all garments need to be lined, of course; some things will be more comfortable without a lining. However, fabrics that irritate your skin certainly should be lined. Linings should be smooth and roomy enough to give comfort when you move. The fabric content of the lining, if different from that of the garment, will be noted on a hang tag or an inside label. Check the lining after washing or cleaning, since any stretching or shrinking of the lining will affect the fit. Pay regular attention, also, to buttons, trimmings, and other details that may need reinforcement after wearing, cleaning, or washing.

How to Know If the Clothes Fit Your Body

Be observant of fit, both in appearance and in feel. A jacket or coat should not look or feel snug over your other clothes. To be sure you have ample room through the back and sleeves, try moving your arms and bending. The collar should lie flat against the nape of the neck. If you will be wearing the collar turned up at the neckline it should turn up with enough width. A jacket should cover the top you are wearing under it, and a coat should be long enough to cover all garments underneath, such as a dress or suit. With pants wear either a jacket (blazer, waist-length, three-quarter, etc.) or a coat that falls below the knee. For long gowns or skirts, a jacket or full-length coat is more appropriate. The coat or jacket sleeve should reach the wrist bone when your arm is bent. When selecting a garment that covers the bust (jacket, sweater, blouse, or dress), it should not pull or gape, since this usually indicates it is too small. There should be an easy fit through the bustline and shoulders.

Tightness Problems Are Common

Skirts should fit smoothly over the stomach. Look at the rear view to check for cupping or dimpling near the hips and seat. If you discover one of these problems, try the next size and have the necessary alterations made. The waistband should be snug enough to hold the skirt in place but not so tight that the zipper or buttons appear strained. If the waistband turns over and wrinkles, the fit is too tight.

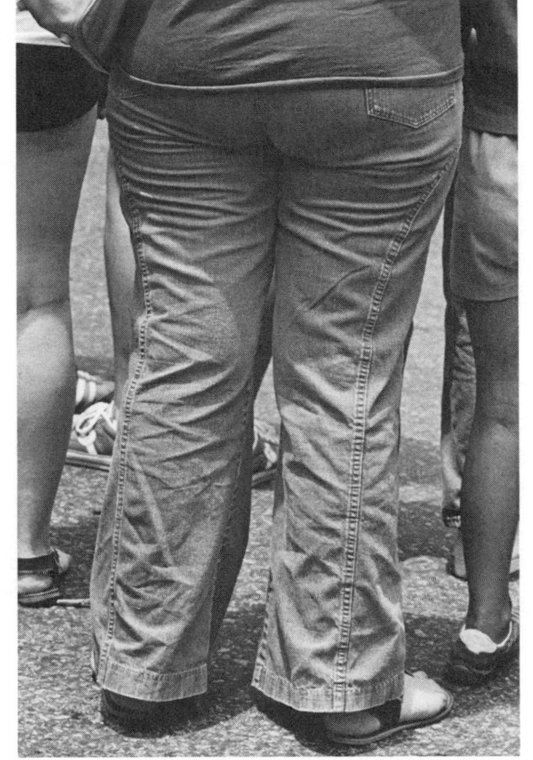

For a proper fit in pants, there are many points to consider.

If it is psychologically important for you to wear size 10 pants, you'll find a pair marked 10 that fits you (even if your size is larger) if you look long enough. Of all the various types of garments, pant styles and brands have the greatest inconsistency in sizing, partly because stores carry both domestic and European brands. In their styling, sizing, and patterns European pants differ greatly from American ones, being cut narrow through the hips, seat, thighs, and legs. Stores try to size them similarly, however.

For a proper fit in pants there are many points to consider. Observe the crotch, hips, and waist. As in fitting skirts, you must look at the rear view. Pants should not cup under the seat. There should be no pull through the hip and seat area. Be sure they are long enough at the hem. It is difficult, for almost everyone, to find a pair of pants that fit well without alterations in certain areas. It is much better to buy pants slightly large and have them taken in than it is to buy a pair too small and let the seams out.

If you find it difficult to buy pants that have adequate room in either the thigh or crotch, a gusset (an angular insert of material) can be sewn into your pants. Have this done professionaly, and be sure it is barely noticeable. This may be the answer to getting that extra inch you need.

If you have gained weight, do not try to squeeze into clothes that are too small. They will fit tightly and attract attention where you do not want it.

If you have gained weight, don't try to squeeze into clothes that are too small. They will fit tightly and attract attention where you do not want it. Buy something inexpensive to wear until you have lost the extra pounds. Usually if something fits too tightly it will also be too short. If a garment has stretched out of shape because of cleaning, age, or weight gain, give it away. Only wear clothes that look good on you.

Lines and Bumps

What you wear underneath the clothes will significantly affect your appearance. When selecting these items, work with an experienced salesperson to assist with size and selection. Undergarments are so varied today that buying the right ones may take as much time as choosing your outerwear. Certain styles of clothing may require specific undergarments for just that style: a strapless bra, straight slip, or pants liner.

For the Foot and Leg

Stockings, pantyhose, support hose, and tights have become important parts of the undergarment wardrobe. You will spend significant sums on these items, so it is important that you buy proper-fitting ones and learn how to care for them.

Pantyhose are becoming increasingly popular because of their convenience and comfort. In 1977, pantyhose outsold stockings ten to one. The control-top style is the best because it gives extra support over the stomach, hips, and seat. Pantyhose have liberated women from stays, garters, and metal and rubber contraptions.

The sheerness of pantyhose or stocking is determined by the denier and gauge. The lower the denier (fabric weight) and the higher the gauge (fineness of knit), the sheerer the hosiery will be. Though many women like different shades of stockings to coordinate with the clothes they wear, I recommend selecting a nude or natural shade, close to skin color, that will blend well with all clothes. If your skin tans well you might need a darker shade. Contrasting hues and patterned or textured hosiery should be worn only if you intend to call attention to your legs. Otherwise keep the shade and sheerness simple.

Hosiery with reinforced toes is stronger but should not be worn with an open shoe or sandal. For my personal use I buy only the sandal-foot style since I find that it lasts about the same length of time.

Tights are similar to pantyhose but are made of heavier yarn and in opaque colors. These can give a handsome look to winter clothes. Be careful not to wear dark opaque tights with a lightweight pale shade of clothes since this moves the eye downward and causes a bottom-heavy, unattractive look.

Support hose are knit from heavier nylon stretch yarns or a nylon-spandex blend. The newer support hose are much sheerer than the styles of several years ago and are seldom noticed as being support stockings. They can be worn every day, all day, or only when you know your leg will need extra support. The lighter the color, the sheerer they look. If you have a leg problem or are on your feet a great deal, support hose are a must. With pants you may want to wear knee-high stockings or socks, but do not wear sheer anklets which show bare skin when you cross your legs. Be very sure your knee-highs do not bind your leg and prevent proper circulation. The newer styles have wide stretch bands at the top to prevent this problem. For extra pizzaz, choose a wild color or patterned sock. K-Mart has a wonderful funky sock selection. Socks can be worn many different ways: turned up, rolled down, or cuffed as anklets. Sheer knee-high hosiery also is available in support strength.

Pantyhose and stretch stockings usually are sized by height and weight. To obtain proper fit it is necessary that your own height and weight fall within the individual manufacturer's size structure. Brands differ vastly so it may take you time to compare different fits before you are satisfied. Both pantyhose and stockings should be long enough in the leg and foot to extend at least a half inch beyond your longest toe. This will give the toe ample room to move, and will prevent tearing the stocking. The waistband should come right to your waist. A stocking that is too short will run because it loses elasticity; if too long it will sag and wrinkle. If your pantyhose run, keep them to wear under pants or boots. If you experiment and find a brand that fits well, stick to it.

Put on and take off hosiery carefully to prevent snags. Wash after each wearing in lukewarm water and mild detergent. Rinse thoroughly. Roll in a towel instead of wringing or twisting. Hang by the toe or waistband with lingerie clothes pins (be sure they are smooth). Dry away from sunlight and direct heat. If you wash them before the first wearing, they will fit more comfortably and excess dye will rinse out.

The Problem Figure

A great many women have the "I'm-not-happy-with-my-figure- (bustline, tummy, seat, legs) but-I-don't-know-what-to-do-about-it" syndrome. The symptoms include repetitive thinking and talking about what is wrong and an accompanying unpleasant emotional state, often a general feeling of frustration. These people hope for magical cures and are susceptible to —

Trying every new diet available,
Exercising morning, noon, and night,

Undergoing painful cosmetic surgery,
Wishing they "looked like her,"
Reading "how to" books and articles,
Checking into diet clinics or health spas,
Asking why they didn't inherit Aunt Sue's legs.
Wearing clothes merely as cover-ups,
Eating two boxes of chocolate — just because,
Blaming themselves frequently.

Some women suffer more than others, and some do more than others to deal with their specific problem. But most don't really know what to do. If you have any of the above symptoms, welcome to the club. There is no real cure, other than accepting yourself as you are. The way to begin is first to accept your figure problems, then buy the proper undergarments for your figure. I am not speaking of a total figure metamorphosis, but of getting help from a garment that can hide a little of that, push up a little of this and tighten a few of those. This is called figure control. In the next pages I will tell you how to select the proper undergarments, what is available on the market, what questions you should ask, and how you should go about finding the right answers.

A Tape Measure Can Be a Friend

If you have the time to do so, make an appointment to be fitted for an undergarment. Even if you have not shopped in a store before, call ahead and ask for an appointment with a salesperson who will be available to give you personal fitting attention. A good salesperson will have a tape measure at hand, since this is the only accurate way to get your figure's proportions. Come wearing the undergarment you most frequently wear, and bring with you examples of the others that make up your foundation wardrobe. Don't rush the process; getting properly fitted and making the correct selections in each category can take hours.

Once a year you should repeat this procedure to take into account any changes in your figure and in clothes and foundations styles.

If you are purchasing a new style in a foundation garment, buy only one or two to take home and wear. Order more only if you are satisfied, because many stores do not allow foundations to be returned.

You also need to wear your undergarments under the corresponding clothes; sometimes they look all right when you are still undressed but give the wrong look under your clothes. Also, certain styles and fabrics in clothes require specific undergarments.

The Bra

Your bra is probably the best place to begin rebuilding your foundation wardrobe. A proper-fitting bra is important not only for looks, it also provides comfort and support for your bosom, back, and shoulders.

There are bra styles designed for different figures and bust sizes and for various clothes and occasions as well. There are many manufacturers and a wide range of prices.

Your bra wardrobe should consist of six bras that you rotate regularly. These six should be divided among two or three different types that are required by certain styles of clothes. For most traveling purposes three bras should be ample. If you choose five bras in a nude or skin tone and one in black, you will need no additional colors. Some of the newer, very sheer nude colors can give you that sexy look you may want when undressed, and also give the right look under your clothes.

White tends to discolor quickly and can look old even when it is still new. Colors and prints, pretty to look at when you are undressed, often show through your clothes. Unless you are wearing something very sheer and want this effect, the color or print will detract from what you are wearing. Laces and other detail also will show through clothes. Lace is hard to maintain, often tears or detaches, and sometimes scratches the body.

Seamless bras are available in most stores and will give you the smoothest lines under your clothes. A wired bra will give good support to all bosom sizes. The old style of boned underwire tended to be uncomfortable, but the new underwire (or wonder wire) is softer and more supple, and shapes to the body. Most bras today are made of Antron-nylon-elastic and spandex in various weights, or Antron-nylon-elastic and spandex with satin cups.

FIT

Many bras are noncling, which prevents them from clinging to your clothes. A wide-strap style gives more bust support and takes the pull from your shoulders and back. Adjustable straps are best to control support and should have some stretch to allow for secure fit. A bra that fastens in the back rather than the front will fit more securely. If the straps rub your shoulders, or if you are allergic to the fabric, plush strap cushions can be sewn into your bra when you purchase it; if not, you can buy them in most notions departments and tuck them under your bra straps.

Alterations are available in many stores to give your bra a custom fit, sometimes at no extra charge. Straps can be widened for better support, tucks taken to reduce size, or more fabric added to increase cup size. Your cup should be full enough all around the bosom. Fiberfill can be added for more cup fullness. Bras that are very expensive often can be repaired at the store where you bought them. Worn elastic is replaced, closures added or replaced, and new straps put on. When you make your purchase, ask if these services are available. Saks Fifth Avenue is one of the specialty stores that offers this service to their customers.

STYLES FOR A FULL BUST

Bra style makes a big difference. For the very full bosom, the oldest and best is by Edith Lance, at $25 to $35 each. The several styles available include the conventional style, the long-line, the all-in-one garment, and the very specialized "P.S.," which is fuller than a double D cup. All of these bras are made to minimize the bosom (for which they are sometimes called "minimizers"). Edith Lance also repairs its bras at a nominal charge when they are returned to the factory. The store from which you purchased the bra will send it back for you. Some department stores and specialty shops either carry Edith Lance "P.S." bras in stock or will custom order them for you.

For the full bust and figure, the long-line bra that comes to the waist and the all-in-one garment gives a smooth, controlled effect. Some long-lines have spiral wiring for comfort and shaping. Fabrics vary, and many of the lightweights give excellent support and control.

Most manufacturers make minimizers, including Bali, Lily of France, and Warners. Because some of these special bras in larger sizes are more expensive, buy only three and alternate them. Add a new one once a year. If well taken care of and washed after each wearing, they should last at least two to three years. I remember that both my mother and grandmother wore their Edith Lance bras for five to six years.

MAXIMIZING

To add fullness to the bustline, a bra with fiberfill is the most effective. ("Padded" was the old term, replaced now by "fiberfilled.") What you want is a natural look with a soft, molded cup that rounds out the shape with the look of a slight lift, adding shape to the smaller bosom. A no-seam bra gives the most natural look.

Is the "not enough" dilemma man-made or woman-made, and who sustains it? The dilemma certainly exists, but what to do about it? I can remember certain teenage friends asking me to save old stockings for them to use as stuffers; in college days I used to look my roommate over to see if both bosoms had been added to equally. Fashion designers traditionally have designed clothes for "the model" look, and most models have small bosoms. It is easier to enlarge a bosom than to minimize one. Consider these points in learning to accept what you've got. Today, of course, surgery can give you almost anything you want. In any case, if you choose the proper fiberfill bra, with some push-up filling, you may find that a little will go a long way and that even a cleavage may appear.

Almost all manufacturers make fiberfill bras. Prices start as low as $4 and go to over $25.

NATURAL-LOOK BRAS AND OTHERS

Most conventional bras today emphasize the natural look with just enough support to keep the bosom slightly supported. The fabrics are very sheer and comfortable to wear. Absence of seams assures the smoothest look under your clothes.

Strapless bras come in various styles. If you don't often wear a strapless bra, you might want to buy a convertible bra. This can be worn conventionally or converted to either halter style, crisscross, or strapless, and can be worn under most styles of clothes. A bandeau strapless bra (a narrow strip of fabric that covers the bosom with slight control) has a sheer, natural look. It gives minimal support, just holding the bosom in place. The bandeau is comfortable to wear and many women use it under swimsuits for a little extra support or under a sundress or camisole top. It has no closures; you either step into it or put it over your head.

The underwire strapless bra gives extra support to a full bosom. The long-line strapless bra gives even more support to the bosom and midriff. The décolleté or plunge bra is worn with very low or plunging necklines. The demi-cup is a half-cup with wide-set straps for wearing under very low-cut garments.

"Nothing bras," sheer and with little support, have been very popular in the last several years. They should be considered as a fashion look rather than a source of support. It is better not to wear these when you are exercising or actively participating in sports. Even if you are small-busted, your breast tissues are helped by support. If you go without a bra most of the time, wear one when you are particularly active. The new athletic bras give you excellent support.

Due to time and change (age, weight loss or gain, pregnancy), your breast tissues may be subject to stress. To prevent injury or trauma to the bosom, good support and protection are vital.

Sleep bras are soft, lightweight, sheer bras for times when you want some support under your nightclothes. They come in many colors and styles. If you are larger busted, it is wise to have some bosom support all of the time to minimize the pull on your shoulders and back.

CARING FOR YOUR BRAS

Did you know that perspiration can break down the elastic used in your bra? That's why it is advisable to wash your bra by hand after each wearing;

machine washing or drying will shorten the wearing life. If you absolutely oppose hand washing, use the "mini basket" that is included in most washers; set the washer on the delicate cycle, using cool water only. Bras with any wiring should only be washed by hand, using cool water and mild soap (cold-water soap is best). Elastic conditioners are supposed to revitalize the elastic. For drying, either shape and hang your bra or lay it flat and shape it, letting it dry away from direct sunlight. Black bras or any dark colors should be washed separately, at least the first several times, to make certain all excess dye has been rinsed out.

Before you wear a bra for the first time, rinse it in cool water to soften the fabric for more comfort.

The Panty

The underpant you wear has an important effect on how smooth your clothes look. You are particularly concerned about panty lines when wearing slacks, and will want to check both front and rear view in a mirror. To minimize panty lines wear a simple brief in nude or natural. The brief should have narrow elastic at the waist and leg, with no lace or other details. Always wear nude or natural color under white slacks, since white panties show through. A trimmed panty is less likely to show through if your slack is lined or of heavy fabric, and is a very loose fit. However, my best suggestion is to save the trims for skirts and dresses and for when you also are wearing a slip.

There is no reason to include colors, white, or prints in your panty wardrobe, although these are all right to wear under lined or heavy fabrics (but not under slacks). One or two pair of black panties can be included, for a color change, to wear under black or other very dark colors, but nude is fine too for these.

A bikini underpant, certainly a sexy look when you are undressed, has a low waistband. It should only be worn under a slip, or with slacks that are very loose and also have the low bikini waistline. Otherwise you will have the waistband of your clothes in one place and the waistband of the bikini in another. If you wear a bikini underpant, be sure the waistband is contoured and fits smoothly at the waist to prevent any additional lumps under your clothes.

Novelty panties include the thong (a minimal panty that covers only the center line of your body, front and rear), the dance pant (has a loose boy leg, often comes to midthigh, and is usually trimmed or patterned), and very fancy underpants to be worn only under certain clothes (usually a full skirt or dress or loose ones that are lined).

The thinner the panty fabric, the less noticeable it will be under your clothes. A panty with a cotton crotch is better because of absorbency. If you perspire a lot, you may find cotton underwear best.

A pant liner is an important undergarment to have in your wardrobe, especially for wear with unlined pants in white or pastel colors and with sheer dressy slacks. It will give a smoother look. Pant liners come in several styles, but I recommend one of noncling nylon, with a wide stretch waistband and a loose leg to the ankle. If you want more firmness, styles made of a heavier fabric with a tighter leg will give more control to the legs, tummy, thigh, and seat. Liners come in white or nude, in various lengths, and are made by several manufacturers. One popular style manufactured by Glydons costs about $10.

The Girdle

For the best figure control, your girdle must fit properly, as measured by a knowledgeable salesperson. Most full and panty girdles are sized small, medium, large, or extra large; or by number: 26, 28, 30, 32, 34. Usual lengths are short (24–26), average (28–30), and tall (32–34). For youthful bodies, nylon-elastic-spandex is the best fabric since it is lightweight but gives good body control. It is available in panty girdles and panty briefs, some of which have a diamond shaped panel over the tummy and sometimes the seat too for extra control. Olga and John Kloss both offer several good styles of lightweight panty girdles and briefs.

For more figure control, a girdle in nylon and satin or double nylon with reinforced panels will give the most strength. These can be pull-on, side-zip, or boned style. For the best fit the waistline should dip in front to prevent rolling. The longer the leg the more control you get for your hips and thighs. Keep in mind that many girdles can be altered. Some stores provide this service in their foundation department. Often a girdle may need to be pinched in at the waistline, or an extra piece of fabric sewn into the garment for a more perfect fit.

To keep the elastic strong, wash your girdles by hand in cold water with mild soap or cold-water soap. Use an elastic conditioner to protect the elasticity. Do not use a dryer, but lay the garment flat and away from direct sunlight or heat for drying.

The All-in-One Garment

There are many styles and weights for this garment. For the figure with excess flesh at the midriff, an all-in-one will give the smoothest effect. If your bust is heavy, choose an all-in-one with an underwire. Double nylon or a nylon-elastic-spandex fabric with tummy and seat panels gives the best control. Vanity Fair and Lady Marlene make excellent styles. Many all-in-one garments are made with a convenient snap crotch. Garments designed for strong control should have three snaps or strong hooks and eyes at the crotch, which may need to be reinforced every few months.

Body briefers, body stockings, and the all-in-one garment give a smooth, flowing, natural look under your clothes, even though you may not need figure control. Lightweight fabrics smooth the figure most naturally. Styles without seams, which are cut on the bias, give the best lines under your clothes. Some newer styles come in colors and can be used for exercising also. Be sure the crotch snaps; some snaps are hidden so you may need to look a second time.

Care for your lingerie items in the same way you care for your bras and girdles to maintain them in good wearing condition. Small lingerie bags to hang on the back of your bathroom door, or near the sink, are ideal for accumulating the undergarments you will want to hand wash.

Slips

Many women are very comfortable in a whole slip, which gives a smooth look and eliminates broken lines under your clothes. Full slips are especially good under knits, since they also act as a lining.

Most slips come in either petite, average, or tall sizes, with a few available in longer lengths for longer fashions. Whether you wear a whole or half slip, the hemline should be the same length as your skirt, especially if your garment is lightweight and you can see through it.

Adjustable straps give the best fit. If you choose a slip with a U, V, or low-cut neckline without adjustable straps, have it altered if necessary to fit properly. Strapless whole slips come in both dress and evening lengths. Some of these have a built-in bra which eliminates the need to wear a strapless bra.

Nude or black are the most useful colors for slips. Lace, ribbons, or other trim on a slip should not detract from the clothes you are wearing.

Slip fabrics should be anticling. Crepe Remarque, noncling crepe, and satin will neither crawl or stick to the body. Tafretta (a new fabric) is heavier and good under knits. Nylon (100 percent) is hot and will crawl and cling. You will find that most noncling slips have a hang tag which says "noncling"; if not, check with the salesperson.

Half slips are available in several lengths, but the most useful lengths for your wardrobe will be the 31- to 32-inch (midcalf on most women) and the 29-inch (just below the knee). Slip lengths change as ready-to-wear lengths change. Most half-slip sizes are petite, small, medium, and large. A slip you may enjoy having in your wardrobe is the "snip-it." On this style, the hem is double-stitched in such a way that it can be cut four times for shorter lengths, if needed. The cost is about $14. A slip that is not lace-trimmed can

New lingerie extras appear almost every season. Choose those that are fun to wear and look good underneath your clothes.

easily be shortened at the hemline, but if there is lace shorten the slip at the waist to save the lace border. If you are very short and usually have to alter your slips, you can buy a slip without a lace border, shorten it, and then add your own trim.

Half slips should be pretty and do something for your clothes. Tiered petticoats can be wonderful in color and lavished with lace. Because they are worn under full fashions, they usually won't show through unless you want them to. Slits at the hem of a slip are comfortable for walking, and if your skirt is also slit these features may come together at just the right spot. If your slip is pretty to look at, you can show it off through your skirt slit.

A long floor-length slip will give a free-flowing movement under your formal wear.

Slips should feel lovely against your body; nylon tricot, crepe de chine, satin, and all the other silky fabrics are the right touch underneath. Pick a style that gives you enough fullness to feel easy and comfortable.

For Extra Flair Under There

Who says garter belts are out? The woman who prefers stockings often wears a garter belt, and so does the woman who wants a bit of sexiness underneath.

New lingerie extras appear almost every season. The teddy is a one-piece underdressing, often with elastic under the bust and around the top to eliminate wearing a bra. It eliminates underpants, too, but be sure you buy your teddy with a snap crotch. These are fun to wear under loose summer clothes; just be careful to buy one that doesn't cause lines under your clothes.

The convertible cami-top makes a pretty liner under sheer evening tops. It usually comes in soft silky fabrics that you can enjoy when they show through. The convertible ones are gently elasticized to be worn either with or without straps.

The camisole and the chemise can be paired with tap or dance underpants. These pants are fancy, silky, and soft and come in a variety of lengths. You won't want to wear these pants with sheer clothes, because the lines will show.

Lingerie fads are enjoyable treats, a bit of glamour underneath it all.

6

Planning a Wardrobe

Clothing seasons can best be divided into a fall-winter season and a spring-summer season.

Go through your wardrobe carefully each season and ask yourself what you wear most often . . . and why.

Comfort should be the foremost factor in selecting any style of clothing.

It has been estimated that only three thousand rich and fashionable women buy all the clothes handmade by the twenty-three haute couture designers of Paris. This is many less than the twenty thousand such customers during the 1940's. Rich women have changed, too. They have become more serious and modern, and though still caring what they look like they are less frivolous with their time and money. You might wish for $10,000 a year to spend on your wardrobe, but this much is not necessary for you to look good and be well dressed. It takes some money to be well dressed. It also takes understanding of yourself and your figure, careful planning and time, skillful shopping, proper clothes care, and some creative flair — which is more important than knowing what is "high fashion." True fashion is not just buying and not just a spectator sport. It is a part of living.

Allocating Your Money

Clothing is a necessary commodity. The average household spends about 11 percent of the total income on clothing. We all wear clothes, and they must be budgeted for. You can learn to dress well on a strict budget, but first you must figure out how much you can spend on clothing. Consider rent, food, transportation, savings, insurance, medical costs, vacations, personal expenses, taxes, and other financial responsibilities. How much do you have left for your wardrobe? On a limited budget you can afford few mistakes and must make the most of your fashion knowledge and buying skill.

Be Dollar-Wise

If you pay cash for your purchases you will avoid interest charges and put a psychological limit to excess buying. Credit cards or charge cards lead most of us into unrealistic spending. Many stores offer a lay-away plan, which will enable you to buy something you might not otherwise afford. Under a lay-away plan a percentage of the total cost is required as a down payment, and the store keeps the merchandise until you have completed payment (three monthly payments plus one final payment). A small service charge is added in most large stores, but smaller stores often offer this service for free. If you find something early in the season, you will have it paid for by the time you are ready to wear it.

Should I or Shouldn't I?

Clothing seasons can best be divided into a fall-winter season and a spring-summer season. It is not necessary to consider four seasons for your clothing needs; you can wear much of what you buy almost all year if you select the right colors and fabrics. Some sections of the country require heavier and others lighter clothing, so before you buy new garments determine your needs. Go through your wardrobe carefully each season and ask yourself what you wear most . . . and why. Is it the color, style, fabric, or the comfort of the garment that you like? If there are any garments you have not worn for the past two years, discard them but take time to evaluate the mistakes you made in buying them.

After narrowing down the things you have left, think about your needs for fill-ins. Do you wear casual clothes more often than dressy ones? Will you be traveling? Are your accessories in need of refurbishing? Will you need new basic items such as a coat, raincoat, or undergarments? This systematic thinking will help you evaluate your needs and costs. Remember to consider your lifestyle: though dressy clothes may be your favorites, if your schedule doesn't require them, keep your choices to a minimum and focus on what you need for day-to-day wear. Too many women fall in love with the wrong clothes and consequently buy items they seldom wear.

How Colors Work in Fashion

No two people have quite the same coloring when you consider the various combinations of skin tones, hair, eyes, eyebrows, pallor or ruddiness, and even pigmented spots. Color and color mixes look different on each person, and color effects also are influenced by how fabric, texture, and design are combined. A number of colors look good near the face on many people. Frequent exceptions to this are black, tans to browns, yellows to mustards, gray, and certain shades of green. Of course this is a very inexact rule and may not apply to you individually. Consider the following examples to see how complicated the problem is. If you really believe that black makes you look dreary, don't wear it near your face. But it's the right color on the bottom if you want to de-emphasize your hips. If mustard or olive-green seems to make your skin tone sallow, don't wear it; however, these colors combined with red, mauve, or pink may enhance your complexion. Brown when worn alone may give you a faded appearance, but perked up with touches of white it can add vibrancy. Camel can have a negative effect on your skin and hair if it is light, but a dark, rich shade of camel may be positive. Gray may be a perfect color for you when it is combined with red.

Colors take on different feelings, too, according to the fabric of the garment. Brown may look dull in cotton but shiny and bright in satin. Olive-green looks very different in cotton than it does in silk.

Remember, too, that colors are used both to attract and to camouflage. Colors can express or affect psychological moods, especially in people who are susceptible to mood swings. Bright red may help you change from low to high, and you may profit by the uplift. On another day, when you want your mood to remain or appear lower key, you may choose a softer, less flamboyant color. Social effects are significant, too (as you know, since a candy-red car attracts your attention sooner than a tan one). Bright colors such as red, orange, apple-green, and shocking pink seem to alert others. You can either express or camouflage emotions. Another kind of camouflage affects the figure. Bright red would never be right in a figure area to which you don't want to call attention.

If you really don't feel good or look good in a particular color, then it shouldn't be a part of your wardrobe. In a pattern or print, one of your least favorite colors may be so subtle that you won't even be aware it is there.

Color Choices for Different Ages

If orange were my favorite color, how would I feel about wearing it when I was sixty-five? I'm really not sure, but I predict I would not want to give it up, even though it was no longer suitable for my coloring. Your figure, your coloring, and your person change with time, and you can enjoy finding alternative colors and styles as your body, personality, and lifestyles evolve and change. Orange may no longer look good on you at sixty-five, but now black does though it didn't when you were forty. Blue may remain your best color always. Good fashion sense and good taste in dressing should be deciding factors in the colors you wear. Some fashion or color choices lead others to conclude that you are obviously trying to look fifteen years younger. The implication is that this attempt is not succeeding. Usually a subtle and realistic approach works better. I remember a woman I met at a wedding who was at least seventy and dressed head to toe in baby pastel pink; even her hair had a pink cast. She drove a pink car and her entire home was decorated in . . . pink. Though she has a trim figure, it was overshadowed by the ridiculousness of her pink costume. Had she chosen a pink blouse combined with a cream skirt, the combination might have been lovely. It wasn't the color itself but, rather, the way she used it that was incorrect. To say that a woman over a certain age should never wear red is absurd. Although a red satin dress on an older woman might be unflattering, a red wool at-home skirt worn with a white wool sweater might be in very good taste. What matters in a garment is not just its color, but its style, fabric, shade, accessories, the occasion on which it is worn, and its suitability to the wearer. Bright red would be a wrong choice for a dress on any woman who is overweight, regardless of her age. Colors don't necessarily have an age limitation, but aging leads to changes which must be individually considered.

Begin With Color

In my lectures I tell women to narrow their wardrobe colors to a maximum of five: two basic or neutral colors and three fashion colors. Most of them assure me that they have at least ten favorite colors and look well in all of them. Although this might be true for a very few people, it is not the best way to achieve an attractive and functional wardrobe. Most of the fashion colors have a multitude of shades and hues, so your possibilities are much greater than the following "Wardrobe Color Chart" suggests.

Begin with two basic or neutral colors, choosing among black, brown, gray, navy, white, beige, camel, cream, ivory, khaki, off-white, tan, taupe, and wheat. The last six are known as "neutral" colors. Then incorporate three more fashion colors that will accent with the two basic colors you have

WARDROBE COLOR CHART

Basic Colors

Black
Brown
Gray
Navy
White

Neutral Colors

Beige
Camel
Cream
Ivory
Khaki
Off-white
Tan
Taupe
Wheat

Fashion Colors

Powder-blue
Turquoise blue
Teal blue
Jade
Aqua

Gold
Yellow
Mustard

Apricot
Tangerine

Rust

Red
Wine (can be basic)
Mauve
Rose

Burgundy (can be basic)
Fuschia
Pink

Plum
Purple
Lavender

Green

Silver

chosen to work with. An example might be: black and tan (basic colors), and powder-blue, rust, and mauve (fashion colors). Combining these colors differently will give you a multitude of effective combinations: black and tan, tan and powder-blue, black and rust, rust and powder-blue, mauve and black, tan and mauve, mauve and powder-blue.

Another set of colors to choose from could be gray and white (basic colors), and red, pink, and wine (fashion colors). Mix gray with white, gray with red, gray with pink, gray with wine. Mix white with all of these colors, or mix pink and wine, or red and pink.

Of course, all colors can be mixed in various shades and patterns. The above principles enable you to narrow your wardrobe colors to combine with your accessories, thus making your wardrobe interchangeable and economical. Each season you may add a new color and eliminate one that you've grown tired of, but usually you will find your favorites and enjoy the ease of sticking with them.

Another way of using color is to try basics for bottoms and fashion colors on top. At times, of course, you can have fun selecting one dress, blouse, or sweater in a special color that hits a mood, but be careful not to do this often otherwise you are back to a rainbow of uncoordinated colors. If you keep your colors to a minimum, the number of accessories can be minimized also.

How often has your coat, raincoat, or jacket color clashed with what you are wearing? When you select a coat or other outerwear garments that you wear often, pick a solid basic color. This assures that what you wear underneath will always look right with what you wear on top. If you decide to add a novelty coat or jacket, then you can freely pick a pattern that will add a more playful or fun element to your look.

When choosing colors remember that you are not matching colors, but coordinating them. Your sweater does not have to match your pants, nor must your shoes match your dress. Your color choices should blend and enhance each other. In the sixties the dyed-to-match sportswear look was the only choice women had for a sportswear wardrobe. Today the color selections are many.

Maximize Your Fabrics

The fabrics you select should be versatile and worn most of the year; otherwise you are limiting their value in your wardrobe. Even though bulky sweaters are your favorite look, they are of little use in a warm climate. Perhaps after you have completed your wardrobe with more immediate needs you can add a sweater as an extra. Most people have problems reconciling their likes with their functional needs and usually buy too many of their likes.

All Garments Have a Fabric, Except the Emperor's Clothes

Before a designer actually begins to design a fashion, he or she must know how well the available fabrics will carry out the desired look. Each fabric, whether natural or synthetic, has special characteristics. Some fabrics will drape and flow well. Some will absorb perspiration, others won't. Some are naturally warmer than others, some easier to care for.

Many fabrics are put through specific technical processes to produce desired qualities. One such process is "finishing," which affects the property known as the "hand" of the cloth, that is, the way it feels to the touch. Other procedures result in water and stain repellency, wrinkle and crush-resistance, and shrink resistance.

The "blending" of fibers is intended to bring together the best properties of each in a single yarn. Also, the desirable qualities of one fiber may tend to minimize the undesirable properties of other fibers. Synthetic and natural fibers may be blended in various combinations. An example of a blend might be 65 percent Dacron polyester fiber and 35 percent cotton. The Dacron contributes durability, wrinkle recovery, shrink resistance, and wash-and-wear performance, while the cotton contributes absorbency. Each fabric manufacturer may use a different name to market its specific product variant.

The most important qualities of a fabric are its look, feel, comfort, and ease of care. If the fabric doesn't have the look you want, don't buy it. There is a definite difference between a quality look and a cheap look, and the *right* look is vital.

A synthetic fabric that imitates the natural material can be used to emphasize the characteristics that are so appealing. Some blends of synthetic and natural fibers closely resemble the natural fiber but are easier to care for. Examples are silk blends, cotton blends, linen blends, and wool blends. These modern textile developments allow textures and weaves to be created which both look and feel natural.

Mixing Textures

Mix up textures, but don't mix up yourself. There are no established scientific principles, only some practical do's and don'ts which work and which also permit experimentation. I've had clients who were sure they should never wear a corduroy jacket with a silky blouse. Yet a wonderful combination would be a gray corduroy jacket and a wine silky blouse and skirt. But tattered corduroy jeans and a silky blouse would not work, however.

Which textures work well together and which don't? I don't agree with those who believe that fabric weight is the main criterion, as I will show. Here are some examples of fabric combinations:

- A satin skirt and jacket will look right with a silky shirt, but not with a bulky wool sweater.

- A wool crepe dress can look great with a jet beaded vest, but a corduroy dress usually looks silly combined with a beaded vest.

- A velvet jumper would look wrong combined with a bulky sweater, but would be fine with a soft, smooth wool or blend sweater.

- A wool tweed suit can be combined with a cable-knit sweater or a silky shirt, depending upon the look you want and where you will be wearing the outfit.

FABRIC CHART

Fabric	*Versatile*	*Shows Wear*	*Wrinkles*	*Fragile*	*Seasonal*	*Day and Night*
Brocade	No	No	Little	Yes	Winter	Night
Challis	Yes	No	No	No	No	Yes
Chiffon	No	No	Yes	Yes	No	Night
Chintz	Yes	No	No	No	No	Yes
Corduroy	Yes	Yes	No	No	Fall/ Winter	Yes
Cotton	Yes	No	Yes	No	No	Yes
Crepe	Yes	No	Yes	No	No	Yes
Crepe de chine	Yes	No	Some	No	No	Yes
Denim	Yes	No	Yes	No	No	Yes
Faille	No	Yes	No	No	Winter	Night
Flannel	Yes	No	No	No	Winter	Yes
Gabardine	Yes	No	No	No	No	Yes
Gingham	Yes	No	Yes	No	No	Yes
Leather	No	No	No	Yes	Winter	Yes
Linen	Yes	No	Yes	No	Summer	Yes
Lurex	No	No	No	Yes	Winter	Night
Matte jersey	Yes	No	Some	No	No	Yes
Mohair	Yes	No	No	No	Winter	Yes
Moiré	Yes	No	Yes	No	Winter	Night
Pongee	Yes	No	No	No	No	Yes
Poplin	Yes	No	Yes	No	No	No
Satin	Yes	No	Yes	No	Winter	Yes
Seersucker	Yes	No	Yes	No	Summer	Yes
Silk	Yes	Yes	Yes	Yes	No	Yes
Suede	No	Yes	No	Yes	Usually	Yes
Taffeta	No	No	Yes	No	Winter	Night
Terry cloth	Yes	No	No	No	Summer	Usually day
Ultra suede	No	No	No	No	Usually winter	Yes
Velour	Yes	No	No	No	No	Yes
Velvet	No	Yes	No	Yes	Winter	Yes
Voile	Yes	No	No	No	No	Yes
Wool	Yes	No	No	No	Winter	Yes
Wool crepe	Yes	No	No	No	No	Yes

Fabric		*Versatile*	*Fragile*	*Easy to Clean*	*Seasonal*	*Day and Night*
Acetate	Yes	No	Some	No	No	Yes
Dacron	Yes	No	No	No	No	Yes
Nylon	Yes	No	No	No	No	Yes
Orlon	Yes	No	No	No	No	Yes
Polyester	Yes	No	No	No	No	Yes
Rayon	Yes	No	No	No	No	Yes
Qiana	Yes	No	No	No	No	Yes

SHOE FABRICS

Fabric	*Versatile*	*Fragile*	*Easy to Clean*	*Seasonal*	*Day and Night*
Canvas	Yes	No	Yes	No	Usually day
Kidskin	Yes	No	Yes	No	Yes
Leather	Yes	No	Yes	No	Yes
Patent leather	Yes	No	Yes	No	Yes
Reptile skin	Yes	No	Yes	No	Yes
Satin	No	Yes	No	Usually winter	Night
Silk	Yes	Yes	No	No	Night
Straw	Yes	No	Yes	Summer	Yes
Suede	Yes	Yes	No	Usually winter	Yes

When you are looking for innovative texture ideas, or texture and pattern ideas, read fashion magazines and be aware of store displays. You will see again that rules you have believed in, such as the prohibition against mixing solids and patterns, don't really hold. You will rarely get a good reaction to a wool striped suit combined with a silk checked shirt, but a small checked scarf tucked into the lapel pocket of a striped suit could be perfect. Good mixing often depends upon the colors you are working with and the size as well as the texture of the patterns. Paisley often combines well with most other patterns if the paisley is small and in a quiet color. Bold patterns, loud prints, large stripes, dots, or checks mix best with solids. Border prints (a design appearing as a border of a garment, at the waistline, hemline, sleeve, cuff, collar, or bustline) create a pleasing visual effect.

PURSE FABRICS

Fabric	*Versatile*	*Fragile*	*Easy To Clean*	*Seasonal*	*Day and Night*
Beaded	No	Yes	No	No	Night
Brocade	No	No	No	Winter	Night
Canvas	Yes	No	Yes	No	Usually day
Kidskin	Yes	No	Yes	No	Yes
Leather	Yes	No	Yes	No	Yes
Mesh	No	Yes	No	No	Night
Needlepoint	Yes	No	No	No	Yes
Patent Leather	Yes	No	Yes	No	Yes
Pigskin	Yes	Yes	No	No	Yes
Reptile skin	Yes	No	Yes	No	Yes
Satin	No	Yes	No	Usually winter	Night
Silk	Yes	Yes	No	No	Night
Straw	Yes	No	Yes	Summer	Yes
Suede	Yes	Yes	No	Winter	Yes
Velvet	No	Yes	No	Winter	Night

There are specific fabrics that can be worn most seasons, day or night, and other fabrics more limited in their functions. Some fabrics are seasonal in most of the country but may not be in Florida and California due to warmer weather year-round. The fabric charts should be helpful in making the right fabric selections for your lifestyle and your climate. Be cautious, but learn to enjoy mixing things.

Some Fabric Specifics

*Challis (shall-*ee). A soft, lightweight fabric without gloss, either solid or printed, usually made of wool, cotton, or blended fabrics. Challis is most popular made into skirts, shirts, dresses, and scarves. Can be worn almost year-round.

Chintz. A glazed (glossy) cotton fabric, either solid or patterned. Worn most often in spring and summer in jackets and sportswear. The term "chintzy" has acquired a derogatory flavor implying cheapness of appearance, but chintz can be used wisely and fashionably.

Crepe de chine. Lustrous, fine fabric, solid or printed, usually of silk.

Flannel. Soft wool or cotton medium-weight fabric, which can be solid or print. Adaptable for sportswear, dresses, jackets, scarves, coats.

Gabardine. Firm, twilled fabric. The finer the weave the softer and duller the surface of the fabric. One of the most popular fabrics for coats, jackets, sportswear, and uniforms. Natural gabardine is made with wool fibers; these also can be combined with synthetic yarns.

Gauze. Thin, lightweight, and usually transparent fabric of loosely woven cotton, silk, linen or combinations of yarn. Used in sportswear, dresses, shawls, etc. Gauze has a natural look and requires little maintenance, but can pull or tear easily. It is usually moderately priced.

Gingham. Washable cotton fabric used for casual clothes. Woven in solids, stripes, plaids, or popular gingham checks.

Lamé. Similar to Lurex, usually restricted to gold and silver. Lamé is seen most often in evening and formal garments.

Lurex. Trade name for a yarn made with bright aluminum foil, in any color but usually gold or silver, inserted between two pieces of colored plastic film. It is woven or knitted into wool, silk, cotton, nylon, or rayon fabrics. For years Lurex was seen only in evening garments, but now it is common to see a cotton shirt with Lurex threads worn with jeans.

Matte jersey (mat). A soft, knitted fabric of cotton, silk, wool, rayon, etc. Has some elasticity. Matte jersey has a dull finish.

Moiré (mwa-ray). Usually silk or cotton, this fabric has a clouded or water-marked effect. Most often made up into jackets, dressy coats and raincoats, and drapery, wallpaper, and upholstery fabrics.

*Pongee (*pon-*jee).* Thin, soft fabric in a plain weave, made of irregular yarns of cotton, rayon, silk, etc. Smooth or slightly rough in texture. Originally ivory or brownish in color, now dyed in many shades.

Poplin. Firm, durable medium or heavyweight fabric in plain weave. Usually made of all cotton or cotton combined with silk or wool. Used primarily for jackets, coats, and raincoats. Can be made into dresses and sportswear.

Ultra Suede. A synthetic fabric developed in Japan that has the luxurious qualities of natural suede plus easy-care characteristics, especially washability. Ultra Suede is used in ready-to-wear garments of all types.

*Velour (*el-*oor).* Soft fabric with a nap like velvet. Used for all types of ready-to-wear clothes and active sportswear.

Voile (vwal). Fine, transparent or semitransparent fabric of cotton, silk, rayon, and sometimes wool. Used for dresses, sportswear, loungewear, and jackets. Can be solid, patterned, or with stripes, polka dots, or checks.

Washing Takes Time and Cleaning Takes Money

Wardrobe flexibility also involves the time and care that must be given to fabrics. First read the care tag and the label in the garment. Washable and unwashable are the two major categories. If the garment is washable, can it be machine washed? If it is not washable, it must be dry cleaned. Washing takes time and cleaning takes money, and you must be prepared to spend one or the other. Remember, also, that some fabrics wrinkle easily and need ironing, whereas others do not.

How to Think About Your Wardrobe

Comfort should be the foremost factor in selecting your style of clothing. How a style looks on you and the flexibility of the garment within your wardrobe are other important criteria. Decide what you need and think carefully about when and where you will be wearing the clothes.

Your wardrobe can be divided into tops, bottoms, dresses, accessories, outerwear, active sportswear, and lingerie.

Make a list of your needs. The things you will wear most often and the basics in your wardrobe come first. These are the things in which you should invest the most money. For example, if you seldom need a raincoat, buy a simply styled coat, one that is either on sale or priced under $65. If your climate requires raincoats often, invest more money in a comfortable style. By comfort, I mean not so full that it is cumbersome or so fitted that it confines your movements or is unattractive over full clothes. Another example: if you wear black slacks very often, buy more than one pair, either identical or similar in style but in different fabrics, one for nighttime and one for daytime use.

Looking at the Outside

What you wear to top off your outfits should be durable, comfortable, and fashionable. Coats and jackets should be selected with great care. These usually are costly investments, and will be worn for several years. For a coat or jacket, pick a basic color in a solid fabric, so there will be no clash with what you wear underneath.

If you are in a cold climate be sure the coat is both warm enough and roomy enough to allow layering clothes underneath for more warmth. A hooded coat is ideal for snow. Don't pick a very light color for your everyday coat, but stick with black, brown, wine, gray, navy, dark neutrals (tan, camel, or taupe), or a very subtle tweed. If the weather is warmer where you live, stay away from very heavy coats with heavy linings, since you won't get enough wear out of them; a zip-out lining, however, is a very flexible choice in most climates.

When you are choosing a dressier coat, the style can be more up-to-date

Coats are usually costly investments. Choose a solid color and a simple style that will look good for several years.

— fuller, more novel or highly styled. A lightweight silky raincoat style may be your best buy, since these are warm enough for getting around by car and are serviceable all year round, unless you are walking a lot at night. Some raincoats in the new polished cotton and tissue weight fabrics have a dressy look, especially in full styles and capes, and can be worn successfully on dressy occasions. If you buy only one raincoat, a trench style will give you the most wear. Buy only a solid raincoat — no prints, stripes, or plaids.

Everyone needs jackets. If you add a jacket each season you will build up your wardrobe. Jacket styles remain fashionable over many years, and can be mixed and matched with your clothes each year to give new looks. No one should be without a classic blazer in either navy, gray, camel, tan, white flannel, black, or a subtle tweed. These can go with almost any sportswear you have. A short jacket (to the waist) is good to have for wearing over clothes that look good with this length, usually full skirts or dresses. Sweater coats, blazers, and most jackets are good weights for cool weather. Dressier jackets for night can eliminate the need for a costly coat. Moiré, velvet, satin, quilted fabrics, and fur are attractive fabrics for these jackets.

A solid basic raincoat will give you the most wear—no prints, stripes or plaids.

By adding a jacket each season, you will build up your wardrobe. Jacket styles can be mixed and matched with your clothes each year to give new looks.

Those Clothes to Move In

Designers have made active sportswear so enticing that you can get an extra burst of energy even before you flex a muscle. Your most important consideration for active sportswear is to be sure the garments are comfortable — unless you don't really plan to "work" in them. You have a lot of leeway in choosing active sportswear, since most styles also can be used as part of your casual wardrobe. But do yourself and others a favor by looking into a three-way mirror before you make your final selection. There are styles suitable for almost any conceivable figure. Heavy legs, large thighs, and a protruding stomach all can be camouflaged by the right selection of styles. (See Chapter 3, "Your Unique Assets and Figure Problems," and Chapter 8, "Special Wardrobes".)

To expand your active sportswear without buying too much, pick three or four bottoms (three short styles and one long pair of tennis pants) then several tops. Your tops should have different sleeve lengths, both long and short. Buy a jacket or sweater in a color to coordinate with your tops and bottoms. Tank tops and leotards can be worn with most pants, shorts, and skirts. These are inexpensive, neat looking, and easy to care for. Cotton blends, jersey, cotton eyelet, and other lightweight fabrics are the most comfortable for hot weather.

Although white is still the most frequently worn color for tennis (usually trimmed in different shades), most clubs allow all colors except very bright ones. Golfers, too, can enjoy all colors. For joggers there are suits and shorts in many fashion styles, shades, and fabrics. In choosing from this wide range of colors and styles, just remember that active sportswear should be as stylish and color-coordinated as the other parts of your wardrobe (see Chapter 8, "Special Wardrobes").

Do Dress in Dresses

Dresses are relatively easy to dress in. If you have not yet learned to trust your wardrobe and fashion sense, you may find the purchase of a dress a good beginning. Try to begin with a new color or style you haven't worn before if you are embarking on fresh wardrobe ideas. Some dresses can be layered — worn with a vest, for example. Layering is both fashionable and functional. Some dresses can be worn alone in summer, with a shirt in fall, or with a sweater for winter months. Jackets and shawls also can modify dresses in a functional way. Dressing is simpler if you can make one garment work for you in several ways.

If you are buying evening clothes, consider buying styles, colors, and fabrics that can be worn year-round. Whether you choose separates or dresses, only buy clothes you love and then wear them a lot. Change accessories to change your look. If the cream dress you like is perfect for dinner, wear it with a sheer striped voile tunic as a mood change for dancing. A cotton print pinafore worn with a low-heeled sandal for lunch will look very different at night if you change your shoe to a dainty T-strap high heel.

Accessory Sense and Sensibility

Accessories make the clothes. If you want your clothes to have the look of something new, and if you want to express yourself differently, then use accessories to accomplish these purposes. The choice of accessories must follow the choice of your basic wardrobe. Accessories are items that increase wardrobe flexibility and change one outfit into many. Make a wardrobe list. Even if your clothes are not new this season, current accessories will update your entire look (see Chapter 7, "Accessories").

When you are selecting shoes or purses, buy them in colors that coordinate with your clothes: black, brown, and neutrals usually can be worn with everything. Some wardrobes may also need a pair of navy shoes if this is a dominant color in your clothes. In warm climates or in summer you should stick to the lighter colors: beige, cream, or off-white. Neutral colors give longer wear than white, which is strictly a summer color for purses and shoes, except in Florida where it can be worn year-round.

When buying shoes, good fashion means comfort and ease of care. You may need several pair of black shoes in varying heel heights and a dressier pair in silk or leather for your nightime clothes. If you wear a particular pair of shoes frequently, a textured leather is best because it will show much less wear and will be easier to maintain. Suede, by contrast, will spot if wet and will quickly show scratches and scuffs.

For a note of fun at a very moderate cost, consider buying some canvas espadrilles. These popular shoes are available in a variety of colors, stripes, or patterns and a wide range of prices, none very costly. (For more on shoes, see Chapter 7, "Accessories".)

Don't buy a purse that isn't functional, that won't carry what you need. The one you carry every day should be large enough, but very big purses are cumbersome and what you want always falls to the bottom. Be sure the purse is easy to open and close. Some purses that are completely open on top are convenient, but things can easily fall out. Your purse fabric and texture should be easy to maintain. A dressy purse need not be too large, since what you carry at night will be less than your daytime needs. A leather or silk purse in beige or black (or one of each color) can go with your entire wardrobe all year. A novelty purse that is patterned, beaded, crocheted, or unusually textured is an enjoyable, frivolous addition. Satisfy your buying impulses in reasonable ways. (See Chapter 7, "Accessories".)

The Wardrobe Pieces

The wardrobe pieces you will need can be divided into two seasons: fall-winter and spring-summer. If you are not on a moderate budget and have more to spend, you will be able to add more garments and accessories than I recommend. Remember, also, that it's better to add things as the season progresses rather than to buy everything immediately. If you choose the fabrics discussed earlier in this chapter, some garments can be worn year-round with only accessory changes. I will describe a basic fall-winter wardrobe, a basic spring-summer wardrobe, accessories and lingerie.

Fall-Winter Wardrobe

Dresses. A challis print or solid that can be layered with vests, shirts, or sweaters. A wool jersey solid that can be dressed up or down for daytime or evening. One dressy crepe dinner or cocktail dress to be worn all year. One long dress in a silky or crepe fabric to be worn all year.

Skirts. One lightweight for fall and early winter. One tweed or small check. One basic solid. An extra skirt in silk, crepe, or velvet for dressier occasions, either long or short.

Pants. Four pair of pants and two pair of jeans or very casual pants. These should include three pair in solid colors and one pair in a tweed or small check. One or more pair in gabardine, of which one pair should be in a dressier style and fabric for evening wear.

Shirts or Blouses. At least six, including four solid and two in patterns or stripes. At least two tops should go with each bottom. Three blouses should be silky or crepe, and tailored. The others can be novelty styles.

Sweaters. At least four to six. One should be a cardigan and the other styles varied. If your climate is very cold you will need more sweaters.

Jackets. Two will add significant flexibility to your wardrobe. One should be a classic blazer in a solid basic color, the other a velvet or tweed in either a blazer or novelty style.

Coats and Raincoats. Pick from basic colors and styles. If you buy more than one of each, consider two different weights. Have one serve as a dressy coat if you do not have a jacket for evening wear.

Purses. One in a basic color to go with all of your daytime clothes. One for evening in either beige or black. One extra novelty purse for daytime or evening.

Shoes. Four pair of shoes in varying heel heights in brown, black, or neutrals. One pair of silk or satin, or leather shoes in beige or black for evening wear and one pair of boots in brown or black leather or suede.

If your shoes and purses are in basic colors, show a wider array of fashion spirit in your scarves, jewelry, hats, belts, umbrellas, silk flowers, shawls, vests, and other extras. This is the place to be free and adventurous. Use an abundance of color, pattern, and texture. How you put them together will be unique for you. An accessory wardrobe should build each year. Without spending a lot of money you can add newness to your dressing and make each outfit into many. Add novelties to your basics rather than the reverse. (See Chapter 7, "Accessories.")

Your Accessories List

Scarves. Have different sizes and lengths and include several in silk, challis, crepe, blends. Have a wool muffler for colder weather. Your scarves should include a mixture of basic and fashion colors, solids, and patterns.

Belts. If you seldom wear belts choose only two in either leather or suede, in black, brown, or neutrals. If you wear belts often, add two or three novelty styles in colors, patterns, and textures.

Extras. Gloves, hats, caps, vests, shawls, muffs, furs, silk flowers, feathers, and decorative hair ornaments are many of the wardrobe extras you can use to express your individuality. (More on Accessories in Chapter 7.)

Spring-Summer Wardrobe

Dresses. In addition to those you can wear all year, add a summer patio or sundress in a print or stripe. A jacket or shawl will make one outfit become two.

Skirts. Three skirts, two very casual and one in linen, silk, or crepe for a dressier look.

Pants. Include your gabardine from fall, and add three or four more pair in lightweight fabrics. Summer white is ideal if you look good in white pants, and these can be topped with a silk shirt for night.

Shirts, Blouses, and T-Shirts. Add three or four short-sleeve shirts for warm weather and at least six T-shirts in pastels or bright colors.

Sweaters and Jackets. Both a lightweight cardigan and a jacket should be part of your summer wardrobe. Choose from off-white, white, or basic colors. If you add an extra one, pick a pastel or bright shade.

Beachwear. If you sunbathe or are frequently near water, at least two bathing suits are needed. If you swim all year round, four suits might be necessary. Also, include one or two cover-ups, one long and one short, to coordinate with your beachwear. Most styles can double as loungewear, too.

Summer Extras. To add to your year-round accessories, consider halter or bandeau tops, shorts if you look good in them, an extra summer-weight shawl, a beach bag, sun hat, summer sandals, and a summer straw or canvas purse.

Jewelry. Two gold chains. Two gold bracelets. Two different styles of earrings. Two different styles of rings. One strand of pearls. Several necklaces, rings, or bracelets in silver. Other jewelry items can include novelty pieces in unusual shapes or vivid colors, such as satin ropes, wooden designs, shells, colored beads, crystal ropes, antique jewelry, and new looks that are offered each season. With some outfits one piece will be sufficient and ideal, with others pile them on.

Lingerie

What lingerie you need depends upon where you set your thermostat, whether or not you have air conditioning, and whether you sit by a fireplace. If your winters are very cold you will want to include a heavyweight robe in flannel, quilted fabrics, or fleece. Some of your nightgowns or pajamas may need to be long sleeved and heavy also. But for most climates and year-round wear, long-sleeved robes or loungewear in jersey, challis, or heavy cotton will be ideal. You should have a half-dozen nightgowns or pajamas to wear during the year, some covered up at neckline and shoulders and others bare. As extra loungewear, think of jumpsuits, caftans, or at-home pajamas as fun additions. A short-sleeved robe for hot weather is a comfortable plus. Most lingerie fabrics are easy to care for, so pick what affords you maximum comfort and in colors that enhance you in your atmosphere. Select a comfortable low-heeled slipper and a high-heeled or wedge mule or sandal to coordinate with your lingerie.

When you are shopping to update your present wardrobe, remember that there are innumerable ways to put everything together. If you wore last year's shirt buttoned at the sleeve, wear it unbuttoned and cuffed this season. Building a multiple wardrobe takes time. Don't rush, enjoy it.

7

Accessories and Individual Touches

The purse you carry every day should be bought with quality in mind.

There is no age restriction for wearing boots, and if a woman over fifty is dressed appropriately, she too can wear a classic boot.

When combining real pieces of jewelry and novelty or costume, ingenuity counts. If you are subtle, no one will examine your jewelry with a magnifying glass.

The most precise way to express your individuality is through the accessories you choose; these reflect your moods, interests, and ideas. Many of us might like the same piece of jewelry, handbag, or shoe, but how you place it, how you coordinate it with what you are wearing, what color choices you make, and when you wear it — these things will make the accessory highly characteristic of *you.*

Accessories are integral to a wardrobe, and whether you are adding them to your present wardrobe or starting anew, you must decide how best to use them to complement your total self-presentation. It is fun to make an impulsive purchase, perhaps while on vacation, but do keep this habit within the bounds of your fashion and financial perspectives. First decide what accessories you will need and how much money you have to spend.

How to Think About Accessories

Try choosing most of your accessories for year-round wearing. Even so, some accessories will be seasonal, such as white enamel earrings, which should be worn only with your spring and summer wardrobe. Black suede shoes will go with fall and winter clothes. You can combine expensive and inexpensive accessories. Why not try a French silk scarf worn at the same time you are wearing a thin two-dollar wooden neckband; or an antique pin hanging from a satin cord?

If you travel a great deal and move at a hurried pace, it is easy to lose an umbrella, gloves, bracelet, or ring. Instead of traveling with expensive accessories, learn how to duplicate "the look" for less money. A five-dollar beige umbrella, brown wool four-dollar mittens, and an enamel pin will achieve the same look as more costly versions of the same accessories. This idea applies to the accessories you wear at home, too.

If you are making a purchase to complete only one outfit (for example, red wooden beads for a summer patio pinafore or a rhinestone belt for a particular dress that you seldom wear), try to keep the cost to a minimum. Good places to look for up-to-date and inexpensive accessories include Penny's, K-Mart, and budget departments in large department stores.

If you are buying a classic accessory to wear for many years, make this a quality purchase. A gold dome ring that you expect to wear every day should be solid gold. A brown leather shoe you are going to wear year-round deserves a larger investment than a suede pair worn only during the winter months.

Most of us enjoy fine jewelry. If your budget requires that you limit the pieces you own, buy classic pieces that will never become outdated. These might be a strand of cultured pearls, a gold or silver chain, or diamond earrings rather than seasonal fads. These can always be combined with costume pieces if your selections are tasteful. Only you will know, for sure, whether a piece is genuine.

Something Old Is Something New

Women have begun to show an appreciation for yesterday's accessories. Many of the newest accessories are also the oldest. Small stores, large stores, jewelry and antique shops, and second-hand stores are offering feathers, furs, hair ornaments, shawls, lace and satin trims, beaded purses, caps, and jackets — an array of imaginative accessories with which to express personal flair.

In addition to wearing modern accessories, women today have begun to show their appreciation for the jewelry and styles of yesteryear.

Comfort Before Beauty

No matter how beautiful or chic an item, no matter how costly or favorably priced, if it is not comfortable do not buy it. Think over your selections carefully. Consider the climate (fur-lined gloves for warmth), the uses for which the item must be suitable (shoes for working in all day), wearer comfort while standing or sitting (not promoted by that wide leather cummerbund), and whether the item restricts action (as would a large ring that prevents you from typing or writing). Unless you feel comfortable you have made an inappropriate purchase. When you buy an item, take time to look at it. Judge the weight, feel the fabric, notice whether it is scratchy or too heavy. Know what you are buying.

Try It Before You Buy It

Something you will be using often, especially when your daily routine is hurried, should suit your needs and function properly. Is the handbag clasp easy to open and close? Is the zipper too flimsy? Does the umbrella fit easily into your briefcase? Do you need printed directions for the belt buckle? (My son's unopenable buckle recently stumped the entire family.) Does your rain hat really keep your hair dry? Will the item be easy to care for? Your purchases should be assets to you, not burdens.

Costly Investments

When making a costly purchase, deal with a reputable store. Then you may take it home for final approval, or comfortably return the item if it is appraised at a different price elsewhere (especially in the case of antique jewelry). If you are buying your first fur or your first pair of diamond earrings, visit many stores before you finally decide. Books, advertisements, consumer guides, and information solicited from salespeople will make you better informed. And don't hesitate to ask friends for advice. There are important differences among costly purchases, and sometimes you will pay for a store's or manufacturer's label rather than for the quality of the item. Get to know the difference. At the time you make the purchase always understand thoroughly what kind of care the item requires and the conditions for insuring it.

Preventive Maintenance

Here are some points to remember before you put on a piece of jewelry for the first time. Pins, especially old ones, may have dull points that could damage lightweight fabrics; if you first run the point over a bar of soap, it will glide more easily into the fabric. Pierced earrings often are tried on by other people in stores, so dip the posts into alcohol to be sure they are germ-free before you wear them. Check all jewelry for sharp edges or rough catches which may snag your hose or the clothes you're wearing. Be sure all catches close properly.

Try to pick colors that are color-fast. Some scarves, hats, and other accessories may fade onto other things you are wearing, especially if you perspire. Ready-to-wear fabrics may fade onto your undergarments, and shoe linings may fade onto your hosiery. Sometimes a label is attached to a garment that says it has been treated to prevent bleeding. If you are in doubt about the color-fastness, and if the item is washable, wash it in cold water (separate from other items) before wearing it for the first time.

Accessories From Top to Toe

Hats can serve a dual purpose: to protect the hair or face, and to add fashion possibilities.

Rain hats in vinyl, rainwear nylon, poplin, corduroy, or chintz will be the most serviceable. They should be treated for soil and water repellency, be wrinkle resistant, and return to shape after being folded in a purse or pocket. These are available in solids, patterns, and many styles. If your raincoat is a basic color (and it should be), then add spunk with your rain hat and umbrella; bright yellow, navy polka dot, or vivid stripes. If you prefer to be more subtle, these accessories can be in basic colors too.

Sun hats should be versatile. You can wrap different ribbons or scarves around the crown. You can also place the hat over a scarf which has already been tied under the chin and add sunglasses for a Hollywood image. The hat should be lightweight and airy. Be sure it sits well on your head and that the crown is not too shallow, otherwise the hat may be blown off by the wind. If you want protection from the sun, the brim should be wide enough to shield your entire face.

Novelty hats are fun and need no color or style restrictions. Depending upon your mood you can try skull caps (knits for daytime, metallic threads at night), berets, hoods, cloches, or simple felt styles.

Hats need not be expensive and should be comfortable. You often will keep a hat on even when you remove your coat, so don't let it clash with what you are wearing underneath.

For the Hair

Whatever you put in your hair will highlight your face and draw the eye upward. Therefore don't pick an ornament that competes with your face or is too elaborate; you will find yourself going unnoticed if you do, contrary to your expectations. Think of comfort. Avoid ornaments that are too heavy and those that don't stay securely on your head.

There are barrettes and combs in gold, silver, wood, fake tortoise shell, enamel, and many colors. You can wear headbands, small silk flowers or ribbons, and at night you might consider large silk flowers, feathers, rhinestone clips, ornate barrettes, and combs or ribbons combined with pins and flowers. You can change your entire self-expression or mood with these details, and your hair style can be changed in an instant for either a casual or more dramatic effect.

An ornament placed close to the face moves the eye there. One at the back of the head (the crown, the nape of the neck), focuses attention on the back or side of the head and emphasizes your profile. You can improvise hair

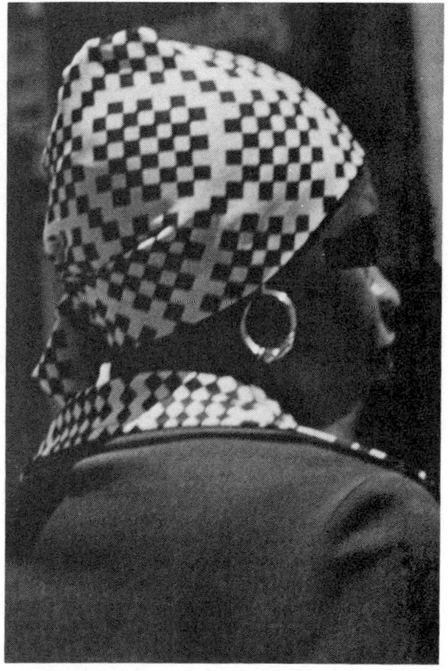

Novelty hair coverings can serve a dual purpose—to hide hair imperfections and add fashion possibilities.

ornaments — a rhinestone clip, for example — by taking a rhinestone pin and putting a hair clip on the back; even a safety pin will work if you twist the hair underneath. Belts and necklaces can be used for headbands, and most things can be glued to the hair for a brief wearing. (Just use a little dab of glue, and make sure that it is water soluble.)

The Scarf

Scarves are always a part of our wardrobe and add a finishing touch to whatever you are wearing. Ways of tying them and wearing them change almost every season. New fabrics and patterns are constantly introduced and shapes are changed, all of which helps you achieve an updated look.

A scarf tied in last year's style is one of the first clues I get to someone's fashion awareness. Of course, the newer look may not become you or please you, and you might prefer another accessory selection. Never follow a trend that isn't right for you; there are plenty of other up-to-date alternatives to choose from.

Some ways to wear scarves are:

As bows — large, small, wide, narrow, soft, stiff; around the neck, under the collar of a coat, sweater, or blouse; tied with the look of menswear (bow ties or knotted with shirts and vests).

Near the face — as ascots in the neck of shirts, sweaters, and coats; untied hanging softly under collars, around the shoulders, around the neck; bowed, draped, knotted, or looped at the ends.

Around the head — bandana style, tied under the chin or at the nape of the neck, as a turban, or as a headband.

On the body — as shawls, cummerbunds, sashes.

Avoid some of the corny or boring scarf tricks such as making a halter top from a scarf or tying a scarf to your handbag.

SCARF FABRICS

Cotton. Cotton gauze, crochet, fishnet, Indian cotton. These give a soft casual look.

Wool. Make sure it is not too heavy or scratchy. Wool gauze, fishnet, and crochet are all soft and airy.

Challis. Cotton or wool. Good weight, adapts easily for day or night. Pretty in solids or patterns.

Mohair. Make sure it isn't scratchy. It sheds easily onto dark clothes.

Silk. Costly, stains easily, unties easily. But silk is very flexible in your wardrobe (despite its drawbacks) and is unmatched for beauty.

Some ways to wear scarves with blouses: as bows or soft at the neckline for a finished look.

Crochet. Very flexible in your wardrobe and a good summer covering. Can be coordinated for dressy or more casual occasions. Excellent for travel when you will need a daytime and evening wrap.

Satin, velvet, Lurex threads, chiffon, silk. These require cleaning. Wear these for dressier occasions.

Blends. The newer fabric blends containing silk and cotton are very effective. Stay away from garments of 100 percent nylon or polyester because these fabrics generally do not have a quality look.

SCARF SHAPES

Oblongs, squares, and triangles (fringed and unfringed) are the usual shapes. The longer the scarf the more you can do with it in draping, tying bows, and so forth. If the scarf is very long it can be used as a muffler with sweaters, blouses, jackets, and coats. Solid-colored scarves can be shiny, dull, textured, or flat. Patterns can be hand-painted, small prints, polka dots, plaids, stripes, scenic, or bordered. Hand-rolled edges give a much more finished look; machine-stitched edges that have been done with care are the next best choice.

Some women are absolutely mad about scarves and want to wrap, bow, or tie anything they have. Scarves can show flair, but beyond a certain point they become ridiculous. Better to leave them off if you don't know when to stop.

Scarves can show flair, but beyond a certain point they are ridiculous. Don't wear a scarf dangling; it is better to leave it off.

Mittens and Gloves

Gone are the days women wore gloves for reasons of etiquette. Today gloves are worn for fashion and protection. They should be worn because they look good and feel good. Nothing feels better against your skin than the smoothness of fine leather. Simple black kidskin gloves are ideal day or night; brown or tan gloves in kidskin, pigskin, or a combination of leathers and fabrics (knit, crochet, or wool) will give a finished look to your daytime dressing. If you have to choose between long and short styles for gloves and mittens, a wrist length is best. Styles can be any that make you happy: lined with fur or flannel for warmth, trimmed with buckles, buttons, welts, and seams. If the gloves are fine leather, they should be cleaned professionally; other fabrics can be hand-washed. Be sure to follow the washing instructions recommended by the manufacturer. To keep leather gloves in the best condition for many years, don't crumple them into your purse or coat pocket or put them away wrinkled. Smooth them into shape, it only takes a second. If you're a frequent caller at Lost and Found, buy inexpensive mittens; a good-looking pair may cost as little as $4. Many stores put their gloves on sale after Christmas, an ideal time to make a quality glove purchase. Give yourself time to fit them correctly. They should fit snug (leather will stretch after wearing), but be long enough and comfortable enough to allow you to bend and move your fingers. Large rings often cannot be worn with gloves; try turning the ring (the clunky part underneath to the palm side of the hand), and if that doesn't work leave the ring off since it will damage the glove and look bulky on your hand. Do not wear your rings over the glove.

I have two pair of white kid gloves, and I haven't worn either pair in years. Unless you are wearing very formal clothes you will probably never need them. Wear beige or black kidskin gloves or no gloves at all.

Tie It, Sash It, Buckle It

Naturally, your first impulse is to pick a belt by the way it looks. More importantly, you must consider how it will look on you and as part of the total outfit. (See Chapter 3, "Your Unique Assets and Figure Problems".)

To downplay your belt or your middle, avoid belts in contrasting colors and nonconservative styles. A belt need not be noticeable to be functional. Understated styles would include: narrow braided belts in leather or suede; thin ribbon or soft fabric ties; thin strips of leather or suede tied or fastened with simple buckles; jute cords; simple canvas stretch belts; contoured belts in quiet colors. A belt worn at the waistline with your top tucked inside is less noticeable than a belt worn outside the top at the waist, or a belt worn below the waist. A simple belt added to your outfit may be just the right accessory for a personal statement.

If your middle permits you to be less conservative, you can tie, sash, or buckle with freedom. Belts can include: wide, printed sashes double wrapped around the waist or tied obi-style or as cummerbunds; wide contoured leather or suede; metallics trimmed with fabrics or rhinestones; clear vinyl; coin belts; straw; striped, printed, or bright-colored elastic and canvas belts; and unique ornamental buckles and hardware on various fabrics.

For great individual effects "play" with your belts. If you wear jeans and a cotton shirt, try a satin belt in a bright color. If your dress is a simple linen, accent it with a soft, print sash. A wool skirt and sweater can be a knockout if belted with a wide suede belt and ornate buckle. The double-wrap belt (or body belt) may look funny hanging on a store rack but it looks terrific on the body. This belt comes in many materials and is wrapped twice around the waist, below the waist or at the hips. Belts can have a great effect on the clothes you wear.

BELT ADVICE

The wrong scarf tied at the waist as a belt can have an adverse effect on your look. A favorite scarf from three years ago, in perfect condition, may not be perfect as a belt for your clothes this season. If you are not sure the look is right, leave it off. Instead, get ideas from magazines and store displays.

A word of caution about belt materials: suede may rub off onto your clothes, and if the inside of the belt is leather or fabric it is less apt to do this. Check suede before you buy it by rubbing your fingers back and forth over the nap. If it rubs off onto your fingers the same thing will happen on your clothes. Some fabrics, such as cord, silk, and straw, will slip and not stay tied even if knotted. Therefore, experiment with these in the store to prevent problems later.

Belt notches can easily tear, unravel, or split if each is not properly bound. Check their strength when trying the belt on. It may be worthwhile, if possible, to have notches reinforced by a shoemaker before wearing. Belt hardware can require care, since silver will tarnish and some gold plate will wear off or peel if it is not of good quality. The salesperson may tell you of any such problems associated with belts of a particular manufacturer. Belt prices vary greatly. A leather belt should be an investment in good quality. For a novelty rope, cord, or canvas belt, you might pay anywhere from $3 to $25.

The Purse

Long ago, purses were carried for holding coins. Today a woman's purse may hold almost anything she owns. When you choose a purse consider in advance how easily it can be carried and the space it provides for what you are likely to carry. Since a purse does not have to fit the way a garment does, the designer can allow his imagination free rein. The style spectrum includes tiny nighttime bags, drawstring pouches on wrist bands, coin bags worn across the shoulder or around the waist, envelope or clutch bags carried under the arm, pouches with handles or shoulder straps, giant novelty bags, and styles that are strictly fashion accessories, such as fur muffs and straw boxes on cord. The crowd of fabrics includes fine leather, synthetics, suede, patent leather, wool, wood, canvas, tapestry, gingham, straw, metallic cloth, lace, satin, antique fabrics, and metal mesh. These may be decorated with beads, embroidery, sequins, rhinestones, ribbons, bows, flowers, and art deco pins.

As a note of individuality you can add your own initials. Don't make them large and be sure they have the look of quality and good taste. Perhaps raised gold letters on black leather, or contrasting stitching on canvas.

DAY TO DAY: MATERIAL, STYLE, SHAPE, COLOR

The purse you carry every day should be bought with quality in mind. A well-made purse will last years and make your original investment sound. If it is not well made and durable, it will not stand up to rough treatment, including being crammed too full.

For daytime use, search out a purse that is refined in style, of good quality, comfortable to carry and able to take you through a busy day and a busy year. If you can afford a leather purse, you may be able to enjoy it for many years. If you have budgeted less for this item a well-made canvas purse with leather trim can have great eye appeal and durability, provided it is well made. When you purchase a canvas, suede, or fabric purse, ask if the fabric has been treated (Scotchguarded, for example) for protection from soiling. If not, buy a can of spray and use it before you carry the purse, and repeat the spraying periodically. This applies to canvas, suede, and fabric shoes as well.

Rarely do synthetics have a quality look. Instead of buying plastic, crinkle patent, or a copy made to look like something else, choose between these: canvas, suede, or a fabric.

Organizer compartments and handy pockets on the inside and outside are additional purse features you might look for. Small pouches, zippered or with drawstrings, excellent drop-ins to hold make-up, pens, or pencils.

I like to carry a large clutch bag under my arm. This style leaves my hands free, is easy to pack, and will even slip into my briefcase if necessary. Because clutch styles usually are not bulky, they are easy to pack when you travel. Many women prefer shoulder bags, but I dislike their weight, which causes my shoulder to droop, and they are not attractive with coats and other clothes

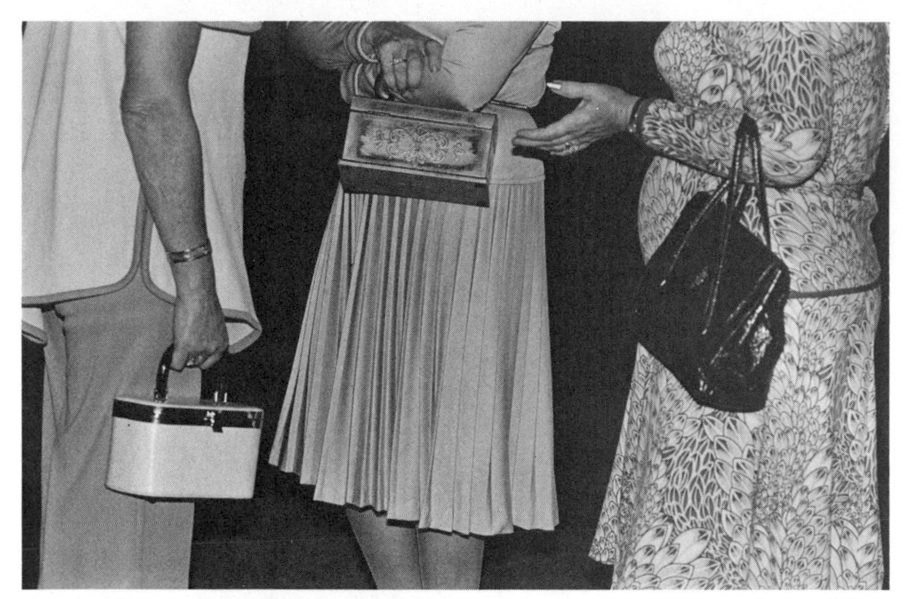

Accessories are integral to a wardrobe . . . you must decide how they will best complement your total self-presentation. With these clothes, the purses are inappropriate in size, style, and material.

that are cut full. If you feel the need for a shoulder bag, try one that can be carried in your hand as well as slipped over the shoulder, with straps that are long enough to go over the shoulder but not so long that the excess gets in the way. Some have straps and chains that can be detached. Handbags for daytime and office can have details such as delicate hardware, slender straps, side pouches, functional zippers, and ornate closures. Remember, more detail increases the chance of repairs since zippers, snaps, and buckles do break.

Purse colors may be almost anything, but keep close to the basic colors for day-to-day use. If you are tired of brown, look for something new in a tonal purse, meaning various related shades ranging from very light beige to chocolate with contrasting trim. Daytime soft shapes can be large pouches, totes, hobo bags, drawstring leathers, or slouchy hunting bags. Others are of frame construction, with the look of attache cases. The softer purse expands as you fill it, and has a more comfortable feel when held close to the body. Others prefer the sturdiness of the frame-constructed bag, which doesn't flop when you put it down and is less apt to fall from a chair or car seat.

Though many purses can be carried for daytime all year round, for a fashion change you might like to switch with the seasons. Leather and canvas purses usually are adaptable to all seasons, but suede, corduroy, or other heavy fabrics are particularly suitable for fall and winter. Spring and summer fabrics include straw and patent leather. Color choices and detail also relate to the season. A cream leather purse trimmed in white, or a navy canvas trimmed in cream — both seem to speak of summer. Heavy leather bags in black or very dark brown look too heavy with summer clothes. If your purse is neither too dark, too light, too heavy, nor too frail, it can be right from month to month.

THE EXTRA PURSE FOR AM OR PM

Novelty purse shapes, fabrics, and designs run to extremes and down the middle. They include small linen clutches embroidered with flowers or trimmed with ribbons, sleek snakeskin envelopes, burlap totes, and cut velvet designs in many colors. Your extra bag may be very casual or you may want something striking. Sometimes just carrying a new purse can make an old outfit feel right.

DANCING IN THE DARK

Express a chic or nighttime feeling by the purse or handbag that you carry. Since the advent of the disco beat, small pretty body bags are a must for dancing stops. Most are designed to be worn either over the shoulder, across the body, or around the waist to stick with you wherever you move. Lightweight fabrics do not restrict your movements. Some are linen, others piqué , mesh, velvet, beaded, or lace. They may be strung with satin cord, grosgrain ribbon, or twisted velvet.

Body bags are also ideal when you are skating.

If dancing is not your thing, then for dinner, theater, or cocktails you might splurge with a purse of tortoise shell, pewter, calf, or black jet beads on silk. If you want to keep your purse budget in line, either buy your evening extra on sale or buy a moderately priced novelty bag.

Unfortunately, I have yet to discover one purse that looks right with everything.

In addition to purses, your carryall wardrobe should include shopping bags, totes, and pouches.

Last year I made an indispensable purchase, a brown shopping bag made of heavy nylon trimmed in leather. I added my initials, too. The uses are innumerable at home and for travel. Varying sizes will carry anything from small packages while you are shopping, to an extra pair of shoes, to running or exercise togs. Styles are never ending. Most are soft enough to pack in your suitcase when unfilled, and others fold up small enough in their own carrying

In addition to purses, your carry-all wardrobe should not be without totes and interesting pouches.

case to fit inside your attaché or purse. I now have several others in different weights (to carry heavier loads) and in fun patterns. Fabrics include mesh, cotton, nylon, suede, and leather. Prices start as low as $5.

Shoes to Take You Anywhere

SHOES FOR DANCING

Whatever shoe you buy, think of comfort first. Except for dancing shoes. I'm now suffering from the morning after: too much dancing or too much heel. The super-high-heeled disco shoe is an exciting look but tiring on the feet and legs. Women's dancing shoes are not made for comfort. The purpose of the shoe you dance in is to reinforce the total outline or silhouette that you and your clothes create.

BACK TO THE BASICS

Black, brown, and beige (including taupe to bone) are the basic and most dependable colors in your shoe wardrobe. White and the fashion colors give much less wearing time, and should be considered only as extras. Navy, burgundy, or gray can be basic if your clothes include these colors. Smooth leathers, textured leathers (calf and kid), suede, and patent leather will be your wisest fabric choices. Also, consider canvas for your sport shoes. Straw

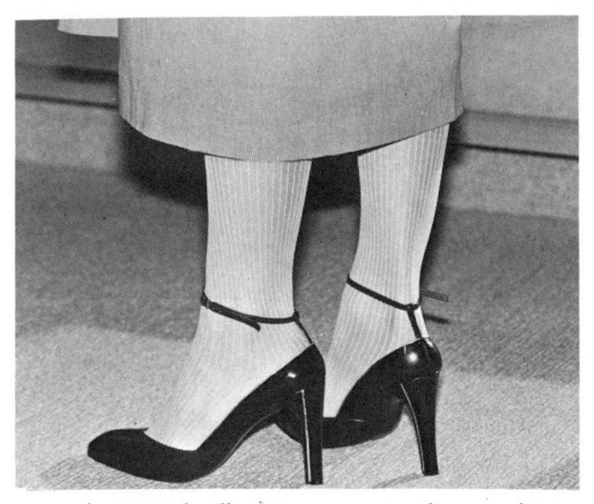

New shoes and silhouettes are significant subjects each season. Basic styles and colors should nevertheless be represented in your shoe wardrobe.

is seasonal, except in Florida or tropical islands. Pick one pair of shoes in black or beige for nighttime and formal wear. If your budget has no limits and you have an affinity for rhinestones or prints, include a print shoe or one with rhinestone accents. Remember, however, that such shoe detail will draw attention to your legs.

New styles and silhouettes will be significant additions each season, but certain basic styles should be standards in your shoe wardrobe. These include the pump with an open or closed toe, the sandal, the well-fitting walking shoe, and the casual shoe either in canvas or leather or a combination of both. Boots also are basic these days and in most areas of the country they still appear in all wardrobes.

BOOTS

There is no age restriction for wearing boots, and if a woman over fifty is dressed appropriately, she too can wear a classic boot. Boots in cold climates are a weather-linked necessity. A smooth leather zip boot is the most classic style. A fuller boot wardrobe might include such styles and fabrics as suede, bright-shaded vinyl, reptile skin, satin (for nighttime), fur-lined lace-ups, cowboy, western, and low-topped pant boots.

If you have circulatory problems, you should not wear boots that come up high on the leg or have a high heel. If you wear boots for long periods of time, wear support hose underneath. Boots are very hard on the legs, though they provide a sophisticated look. When you wear boots with skirts or dresses, make absolutely sure your hem definitely *covers* the top of the boot. Your bare leg should never show. Fashion boots can be short, provided you wear opaque or textured stockings with them.

Boots with pants can be worn in numerous ways. Pants can be worn covering the boot, tucked into the boot, cuffed over the boot, and knee socks or stockings (textured or opaque) can be exposed between the pant and boot.

THE ESPADRILLE

This shoe, canvas with a hemp wedge, is a classic today. Canvas footwear has become acceptable for year-round wear, except in extremely cold climates. Canvas is a right fashion look at a right price, beginning around $24.

SANDALS, CLOGS, AND WEDGES

Sandals produce a silhouette effect, often very feminine, very high heeled, and very open. They may have an ankle strap or ribbons tied around the leg; they can be the sexy sling style — open or closed toe with a strap fastening around the heel. The slide, sling or mule with a high heel is a favorite

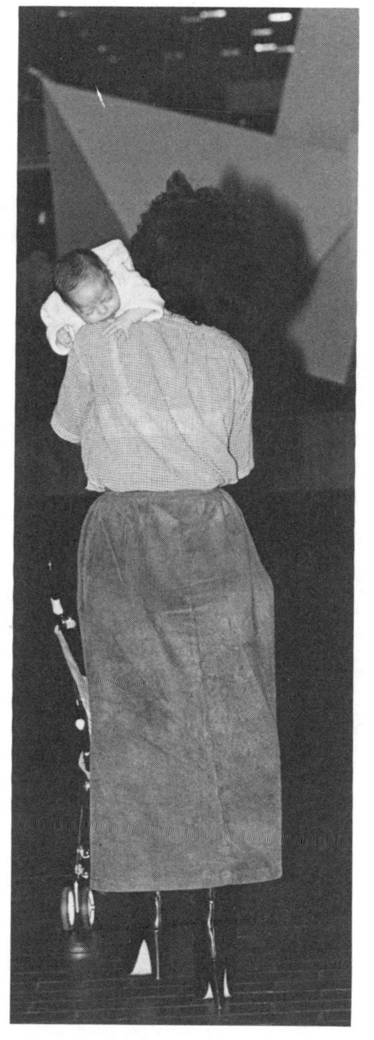

When wearing boots, the bare leg should never show. Boots can be short if opaque or textured stockings show between the skirt hem and boot top.

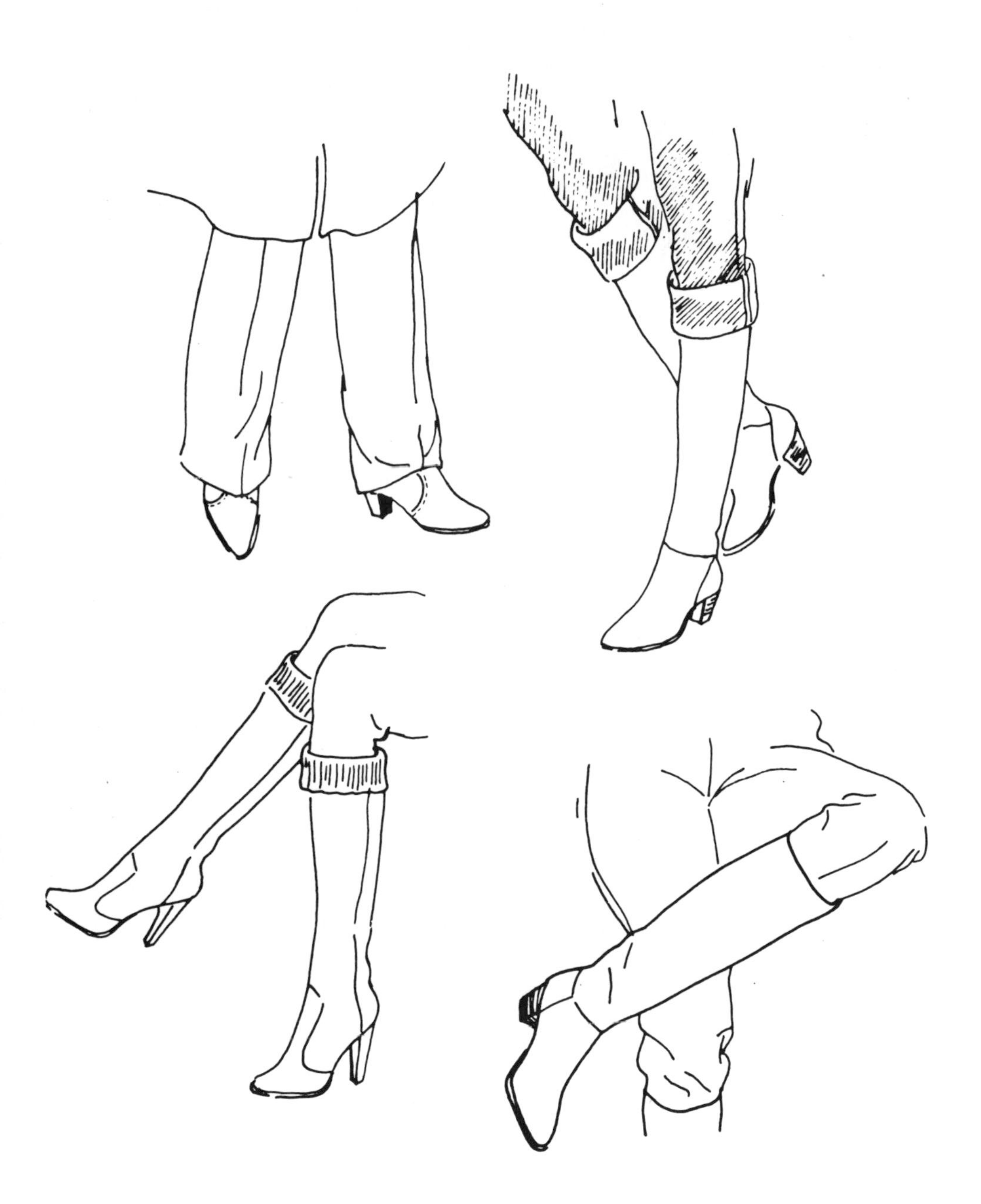

Boots and pants can be worn in numerous ways.

with jeans and nighttime dressing but is inappropriate for business attire. To assure comfort, practice walking in them at home. A casual sandal may have a crepe or hemp platform sole or be very flat for summer wear. Sandal fabrics include satin, silk, peau de soie, leather, suede, reptile skin, canvas, straw, and clear plastic.

Many people still love clogs, which make good jean or beach shoes though they are not ideal for most clothes. They are an adaptation of the Dutch wooden shoe, and either you love them for comfort or you'll never find them comfortable.

Be cautious going up and down steps while wearing a high wedge or clog. These styles are fun and can look good, but keep your orthopedist's number handy.

ESTHETICS OF SHOES

Why do most shoes come to a point in front? As with many fashions, shoes are used to create an illusion. Our feet don't come to a point in front, but traditionally our culture prefers pointed shoes because they make the foot look slim and elegant. The earliest shoe, a sandal woven with papyrus leaves, was introduced primarily for fashion, it is thought, since papyrus is a poor choice for protection. Today at least 80 percent of all footwear is bought primarily for fashion, not for comfort and protection.

High heels create a long, leggy look and add contour to the leg by causing contraction of the calf muscles. By general agreement, high heels add sensuousness to the look and movement of a woman, however unsound they may be medically.

Although your eye will choose a shoe for looks, your feet require shoes for comfort. If you are on your feet a lot, go with comfort first. You will get the most leg and foot support from a sturdy walking shoe, such as a crepe-sole leather with an excellent lining. For touring, a sturdy lace-up with crepe sole is best.

When buying shoes for comfort don't select a style so heavy or bulky that your feet will have to drag them around. Also avoid unconstructed and frail styles that give no support at all.

The continuing comfort and life of a shoe depend on its quality and construction. Shop around until you are sure you have found a comfortable shoe. Feel it in your hand. Is the material soft and supple? Will it bend with your foot? Does it really fit properly or are you trying to prove something? Is it wide enough, and what about the length? You want ample room for your toes, but the shoe should not be so wide that it gapes on the sides and looks and feels sloppy.

As in buying anything, if you find a brand that looks good and is comfortable, keep this name in mind each time you buy new shoes. Though styles change, manufacturers often use the same lasts for sizing. Be flexible in choosing a shoe size: in one brand or style you may wear size 7 but in another a size 7 1/2. Before you buy the shoes, walk around in them as much as possible in the store and use the mirror at all angles. When you get them home, repeat this procedure. Never wear shoes for the first time when you are away from home or when you will be walking or standing a lot. A foot is a delicate piece of living machinery. It is where the body takes its stand, so take good care of it.

When you want to change shoes during the day and are away from home, carry your extra pair in a shoe tote. Totes are available in canvas or leather, and some will hold more than one pair of shoes.

If your lifestyle is such that you sit much of the time or wear shoes for only a short time, this is when you can think "fashion first."

There is an advantage to wearing pants when you want the most comfort for your feet. The right pants length will camouflage your feet and permit you to wear an old, well-worn pair of shoes. Select a dark colored shoe and pant; your shoes will go unnoticed and your feet will be pampered.

PLAYING DOWN LEGS

Do you want your legs to stand out? If not, keep shoe colors dark with dark clothes. Wear cream or beige, not white, with light clothes. The silhouette should be a simple one. Boots are a good leg camouflage, too, but if you are trying to cover a skinny leg you may spend all season looking for a pair that will stay up on your leg. Try wearing two pair of heavy knee socks to fill out the boot. Select a classic boot style in a dark color.

In all styles of shoes be conscious of heel height. A very low heel is not as dressy as a higher one.

Mix or contrast shoe fabrics with the clothes you wear. For example, if your dress is wool crepe, wear a suede or smooth leather pump for daytime and switch to a silk or satin shoe at night. The color of the shoes and clothes may be the same or different, but the fabric mix is a more effective way to make a fashion statement.

HOW MUCH, PLEASE?

The price of shoes will vary, not only by brand but according to when and where you buy them. Buy shoes on sale to help your budget. Mid-May to late June, and Thanksgiving to Christmas are shoe sale months in many cities. Discount shoe stores, often specializing in designer names and hard-to-fit sizes at lower prices, have become very popular. As with all discount stores, know the store policies. If you can buy the best for less, why not?

Do you want your legs to stand out? If not, wear cream or beige shoes with light colors. The shoe silhouette should be a simple one.

Canvas and straw shoes often cost less than $20. Other shoes may average $35 to $65, with designer shoes going over $100. Well-made leather or suede boots begin around $65 and go as high as $175 to $200.

MORE SHOES

Shoe extras are many: shoes for hiking, running, walking, athletics; specially designed shoes for problem feet; custom-made shoes that mold to the foot for extra support and comfort; all-weather styles (galoshes or rubbers). To get the best selection and fit in these specific types of shoes, go to stores that specialize in selling them. Bedroom slippers, moccasins, Topsiders

(Sperry), a leather moccasin with a rubber sole — and beach shoes should all have their place in your shoe brigade.

SHOE CARE

Get into the habit of keeping your shoes in good wearing condition and they will last much longer. Here's how:

Spray shoes and boots, when they are new, with a water and soil repellent. Different types are available for suede, leather, and fabrics. Repeat this spraying periodically. To touch up the nap on a suede shoe use a shoe brush, brushing lightly over the spot in a circular motion. Suede nap will often wear off and look dull, and a professional shoemaker may be able to dye the specific area or the entire shoe to revive the color. If this can't be done, the pair should be discarded. Smooth leather can be touched up with polish to hide scuff marks and scratches. If you want to do this yourself, use paste wax applied with a soft cloth. Liquid polish is hard to control and tends to drip on areas you don't want to polish. Patent leather can be kept glossy with patent spray, a damp cloth, or Vaseline applied with a soft cloth.

To keep the shoe in shape, use shoe trees (metal, plastic or wooden foot molds). Boots keep their shape best when you put them away with boot trees or small sand- or lead-filled bags in the feet; these also prevent them from falling over in your closet. Keep your boots at their finest with periodic visits to the shoemaker, who can polish and touch them up to assure more years of wearing. Wet boots and shoes should be dried immediately to prevent spotting and streaking. Stuff them with newspaper or insert shoe or boot trees when they are damp so that they will retain shape. Soles, heels, and shoe linings can be touched up professionally if damaged by water or other causes. For some reason we overlook shoemakers these days, but going to a good shoemaker can save you time and money. Unless you are certain how to care and repair, leave it to the experts.

BUTTONS, BOWS, ZIPPERS, STRAPS, AND STONES

Most ornaments can be reglued if they fall off. Shoe straps can have additional notches added for better fit and any excess fabric cut off. It's wise to have the notches reinforced to prevent splitting or stretching of the strap.

Boot zippers usually can be replaced, but try to use breakage prevention methods when zipping your boot. Be sure no boot or hosiery fabric is touching the zipper, then use your finger to guide the zipper up and down. Avoid zipper strain by either pushing the boot down below your calf and slowly bringing it up as you zip, or guiding the boot material with one hand and the zipper with the other.

Remember to alternate your shoes. Do not wear the same pair day after day, because the materials need time to breathe and be cared for, just as with your clothes. Also, if you are on your feet many hours, switch shoes once or twice during the day.

Jewelry, the Talking Ornaments

Nothing should be more distinctive in your wardrobe than your jewelry. This is an absolute way of expressing yourself — your individuality, your mood, your creativity. Think of your jewelry as part of a collection that will last and will be added over the years. Regardless of cost, most of the time each piece will be a long-term wardrobe investment and signify enduring aspects of yourself. If something you choose is very inexpensive, this purchase might last only briefly but be just what you need to achieve an ideal look.

Jewelry can be divided into three catagories: fine (real), costume, and novelty. It is perfectly acceptable, interesting, and innovative to mix any of these types. For example, a strand of pearls may be combined with a satin choker. Even fashion authorities and fine jewelers have become more flexible in their attitudes toward combining all sorts of jewelry, including gold and

Your jewelry should be distinctive and tasteful. The pearls worn this way tell us that the woman has both taste and flair.

silver. Even if certain fine pieces are not affordable, a costume or novelty piece often can create the same impression or an even better one.

Fine (real) jewelry is made of silver, gold, platinum, or a combination of these metals and may or may not be adorned with precious or semiprecious stones or pearls. Fine jewelry should have lasting quality, esthetic design, and intrinsic value.

Costume jewelry is made of nonprecious metals often with semiprecious or imitation stones. Some pieces, however, can be very costly.

Novelty jewelry refers to costume pieces with novel shapes, designs, and materials such as shells, rope, and fabrics; it is usually not too costly.

QUESTIONS OF TASTE

Some pieces of jewelry are so important alone that they should not be combined with others. Some pieces can be worn alone or mixed with several other pieces. For example, a large cameo brooch on a stiff gold neckband might say more alone than if it were worn with several gold chains. A gold chain would be more interesting combined with other chains of several lengths and with a strand of pearls; the gold and milky pearl color work to light up the face.

When combining real pieces with novelty or costume jewelry, ingenuity counts. If you are subtle, no one will examine your jewelry with a magnifying glass to find out if it is stamped 14k or not. But if you're passing off a huge piece of glass as a diamond, it might well be scrutinized. Wear your jewelry with good taste as well as good judgment. If you choose materials that are not costly, such as ribbon, shells, or glass beads, the commercial value is insignificant compared to the look. If you don't want to spend the money for a strand of pearls, either select a very good imitation or make another jewelry choice. An inexpensive gold lookalike may turn black and the gold wear off; if this happens, don't wear it. Chances are you have gotten your money's worth.

Very ornate jewels should be saved for wearing with your wardrobe finery. It is rarely good taste to wear these pieces during the day, except on special occasions. I believe that fine jewelry for daytime wear should be simple, but pearls, solid gold, and less flashy pieces can be worn tastefully day or night.

Other metals are becoming important in jewelry, including brass, copper, pewter, metal wires, and chrome. Substances such as clay, sand, lucite, mesh, synthetic versions of tortoise shell and ivory, and even pumpkin seeds figure in new jewelry ideas each season.

Some pieces of fine jewelry are trendy and may not present lasting esthetic value. These include diamonds by the yard, hanging diamond monograms (hanging from rings, necklaces, and bracelets), and gold astrological signs on chains. Trends generally are short-lived and not worthy of large investments. Do you remember the very costly sterling-silver-and-turquoise phase? I had friends who spent hundreds of dollars on these pieces several years ago and never wear them now. Remember, you can duplicate a faddy look (if fads are your fun) with less costly pieces.

Gold jewelry is defined by its Karat content, the percentage of gold alloyed (mixed) with another metal. Alloys are used because pure gold is too soft for jewelry. The usual Karat designations are 22K, 14K, 12K, and 10K. The higher the Karat number, the higher the percentage of gold and the higher the price. The term "gold filled" means the piece has an outside layer of gold over a less expensive metal; it should be much less costly than the above.

To care for your gold jewelry at home, store each piece individually, or in divided drawers or containers. Be sure you wrap or place it in something soft. Velvet, chamois, or satin are ideal. To keep gold clean and bright, wipe it with a damp cloth or a chamois cloth. Never use silver polish on gold.

Silver jewelry, like gold jewelry, can be either handmade or machine-made. Because silver is less expensive than gold, more people work with silver in handcrafting jewelry pieces. Silver tarnishes and is hard to clean and keep bright, so take time to keep it shiny by using either a treated chamois cloth or silver polish. To store silver, wrap it in Pacific cloth or keep it in drawers lined with Pacific cloth, which will keep tarnish to a minimum.

Genuine pearls are formed naturally inside a living oyster as it reacts to a natural irritant. *Cultured pearls* are started by inserting a bead into an oyster, to which the animal reacts in the same way, by growing an outer skin of nacre (a shell-like substance) around the bead; a cultured pearl has the luster and color of a genuine pearl. *Imitation pearls* are glass beads covered with a paint containing ground fish scales.

The price of pearls is affected by several factors: whether they are genuine, cultured, or imitation; their size, shape (round or baroque), clarity, smoothness, color; how many there are and how well they are matched in the piece of jewelry. Most strands of pearls come in one of three lengths: choker (14 1/2 – 16 inches), matinee (28 inches), or opera length (32–36 inches).

You can add practical and fashionable nuances to your strand of pearls by using a pearl shortener to change the length of the strand. The shortener is a small pin-like device — pearl, gold, or jeweled that can be hidden at the nape of the neck or shown decoratively at the side or front of your pearls. Pins, too, can be thought of as additional pearl adornments. Bring both sides of the strand together with an ornate pin in front, or attach a pin to either side of the strand.

To care for pearls, wash them with a damp cloth and do not soak or boil. When you see the thread begin to discolor or lose shape the pearls should be restrung by a professional jeweler. Store pearls in a soft individual container or pearl bag, or wrap them in velvet or chamois cloth.

Don't wear jewelry containing stones when you are cooking, since stones can be damaged by substances such as salad dressing. To clean stones, wipe them off or use a very soft brush; do not immerse in hot water. Jewelry with stones should be stored individually or in lined drawers to prevent scratching. Be careful of perfume, which can damage stones and pearls.

Antique jewelry is valued according to the date and beauty of the piece, the type of stones, and the type of metal used. Antique pieces have become more and more popular today and are enjoyed for their unusual designs and individual charm. If you want to invest in a costly piece, deal with a reputable shop. Otherwise try your luck with garage sales, flea markets, and auctions. Something old and inexpensive may even be a valuable find.

WATCHES ARE JEWELRY TOO

A fine *watch* can be considered jewelry and should last for years if cared for properly. If the watch requires winding, do this once a day, preferably in the morning before you put it on. If you have it cleaned every two years, it could last forever. Despite what fashion authorities may say, watches can be worn with formal attire providing the watch style is consistent with your dress. Digital watches can be extremely reliable and accurate. Buy a watch from a jeweler who will include a guarantee and provide good care and service on the parts.

Some inexpensive fashion and novelty watches are superb in design, but I've had little luck with their reliability. Most jewelers do not want to service novelty watches; you must send them back to the factory for repair, and you may wait months for the job to be done. So, while I advocate their good looks, I have become reluctant to encourage their purchase.

EARRINGS: STYLE, SHAPE, COLOR, MATERIALS

Clip-ons clip over the ear lobe. *Screw-ons* screw onto the ear lobe. *Pierced* styles insert into a tiny hole in the ear lobe and are suspended by a metal loop, ring, or stud; they are less likely to be lost. Many styles must be removed when talking on the telephone. Studs can push out of the ear and are sometimes uncomfortable. If you want pierced ears I suggest this be done in a doctor's office. Wear solid gold posts to prevent inflammation. The new magnetic earrings give the look of pierced earrings, but are held close to the ear by a magnet rather than by a post or loop through the lobe. Try these as an alternative to piercing.

Button earrings fit close to the ear, vary in size from tiny to more than an inch, and are made of every type and combination of material. A *drop, loop, or pendant* hangs below the ear lobe, and can be simple or elaborate in design. A *stud* is an ornament fitting close to the ear, such as a diamond or pearl, usually attached to a gold post. *Novelty earrings* come in a multitude of shapes, designs, and materials, such as shells, animals, flowers.

Earring shapes can be used to alter the shape of the face. A long suspended design adds length: keep it lightweight, however, or the face will look weighted down or droopy. A fat, wide, or round design adds width. If your hair is long, you can expose the earring by pulling the hair away from the face, or by wearing an earring longer than the hair or large enough to be seen when you move your head.

Earring color can add either life or dullness to your face. If you are dressed in dark colors or monotones, brighten your face with gold, red, white, bone, or silver earrings. Pearls add brightness to redheads and brunettes and softness to blondes and look particularly soft and elegant on women with gray hair. All these women look attractive in silver and the same is true of gold on women with gray hair. If your hair is streaked with blond or heavily bleached, don't choose a brassy gold that will compete with your hair color.

Materials are varied and can be handmade or machine-made. Tiny beads, unusual cameos, lucite balls, ivory, jade, coral, diamonds, and almost any other imaginable stone can be set into gold or silver for the right touch at the ear. Wearing an earring adds a finished look. A dramatic earring is large and elaborate. If you are tall enough to carry the look, great; otherwise be less ostentatious and go small. If you wear glasses, your earrings should be simple and not too large.

The Necklace

Necklaces — from tiny individual chains to magnificent large stones hanging around your neck — can reflect a thousand moods. Each one, or many hung together, will permit you and your clothes to say something different. Chains can vary in length from choker style to waist length. You can combine beads with pearls, silver pieces with gold, chains with pendants hanging from them, stiff neckwires (those that are hinged will lie flattest against the neck) with ropes of hemp.

How you wear necklaces can enhance your face and figure. If you want attention focused near your face, the necklace should be choker length or should hit the collar bone. Necklaces and pearls are a grand way to hide neckline wrinkles or fill in open necklines. If bustline attention is important, the necklace should hang to the cleavage. You don't want competition between the necklace and your clothes. If your clothes are patterned or busy with detail, make your necklace simple. If you're wearing solids, choose a piece that will add interest to your total look. If the fabric is lightweight, don't wear a heavy necklace that will interfere with the soft folds of the fabric. If you are wearing an outfit detailed with bows, lace, pockets, and other extras, omit the necklace unless it is very thin. Switch necklaces, and wear them alone or combined differently each time you accessorize.

The Pin

Pins are prominent in fashion. Whether yours are old or new, wear them. Both bar pins and stick pins can be worn alone or scattered with several others. Place them on collars, pockets, at the hip and waist, on cuffs or wherever you want attention. Cameo pins still are classic beauties, worn around the neck or pinned. Art deco pins — the authentic and the not-so-authentic — can make positive comments. Pins of colorful plastic, flowers, enamel, wood, ivory, and horsehair will make what you wear a very individual personal expression.

If you want to be able to wear your pin as a necklace too, ask your jeweler to add a tiny loop to the pin that will attach to chains or a neckwire.

Don't wear pins that are too heavy for the fabric you are wearing. Dainty pins should be placed in just the right place if the fabric is heavy: try the edge of the shoulder or very near the neckline. Use a safety lock on your costly pins, and remember to remove the pin from your clothes before you put them away, wash them, or send them to the cleaners. Eliminate pins unless you are sure they are becoming to you and to your clothes.

Bracelets

Bracelets are an important added touch, and like earrings they give a complete look to your dressing. There are some simple and comfortable designs that you will enjoy wearing every day. I have two thin gold chain bracelets that I almost never take off. Whether I'm in a hurry, swimming, or on the tennis court, I have that touch of gold at hand. Enamel combined with silver, wood combined with unusual plastic shapes, diamonds sprinkled on gold mesh, mother-of-pearl and antique platinum are all excellent combinations for bracelets.

Designs include bangle styles, such as continuous hard loops or hinged bangles that open and close. The hinged bangles are easier to fit onto the wrist. Other styles include mesh, chains, braided metals, twisted fabrics, wide and narrow cuffs and the well-remembered charm bracelet.

For a simple understated look, wear one or two bracelets at a time. When in the mood, combine many on both wrists. Some of the newer chinoiserie lacquer designs have wide cuffs that attract much attention. For safety, a figure-eight catch is usually best and won't snag on your clothes and other fabrics.

Rings

Rings become a focal point of the hand and fingers and should be kept simple and few, unless you particularly want to call attention to them. Designers have crafted rings by machine and by hand in every conceivable material and design. Besides the rings we wear for their symbolism — engagement and wedding rings, signet rings — there are cocktail and dinner rings, cluster rings (stones set in groups), pinky rings (worn on the fifth finger) and other styles. The vogue for a ring for every finger has now passed. Though you may enjoy combining them, leave ten at once to Sammy Davis, Jr.

A Basic Jewelry Wardrobe

Earrings. Two pair of earrings in different shapes, at least one gold and the other pearl, silver, or colored stone (jade, opal, etc.) Several inexpensive costume or novelty earrings, such as white enamel loops, red buttons, or lucite squares for summer wear. There are good choices of costume earrings for nighttime wear, either very simple or novel for a more faddish flavor. Whatever you choose they should be interesting, not corny.

Necklaces. Two gold necklaces or chains of different lengths. One strand of pearls; if the length is at least 30 inches you will have more flexibility by sometimes using a pearl shortener. One pearl shortener, plain or with pearls or stones. Cost begins around $25 at most jewelry stores. One strand of colored beads, either jade, coral, or wood. Several novelty ropes of varying lengths in satin, velvet, or hemp.

Bracelets. Several gold and silver bracelets, in varying widths, to wear separately or combined. Several novelty bracelets in wood, lucite, plastic, or beads. Two dressier bracelets in pearl, stone, or enamel, which can be worn alone or combined with gold and silver.

Rings. Four or five rings which can be worn alone or interchanged in gold, silver, wood, stones, or lucite.

Pins. Three gold pins different in style and shape, such as bar, stick, or novelty possibilities. Three novelty pins in plastic, enamel, stones, and the like.

What's right in jewelry is related to the way you wear it. Here is a specific jewelry combination:

Jade stud earrings
Strand of choker-length pearls
Strand of 18-inch jade beads
Thin gold bracelet
Wide mother-of-pearl cuff bracelet
Gold dome ring
Silver and pearl pinky ring

This combination is right day or night. The jade color and pearl luster introduce color around the face.

Consider another combination:

Red wooden button earrings
Two satin ribbons, red and yellow, twisted at the neckline
Two thin wooden bangle bracelets
Yellow enamel ring
Wooden pinky ring

These jewelry combinations are ideal for summer wear; the pieces could cost less than $15 all together.

Look at this group of jewelry items:

Enamel drop earrings in blue and green
Enamel and diamond pin attached to a gold neckwire
Gold mesh bracelet
Diamond band worn on pinky finger

These combine color with simple elegance.

Still another set:

Sleek silver and brass drop earrings
Large Indian-head pin, worn at the center of the collar bone
Six brass and silver thin bangle bracelets
Two antique silver and gold rings

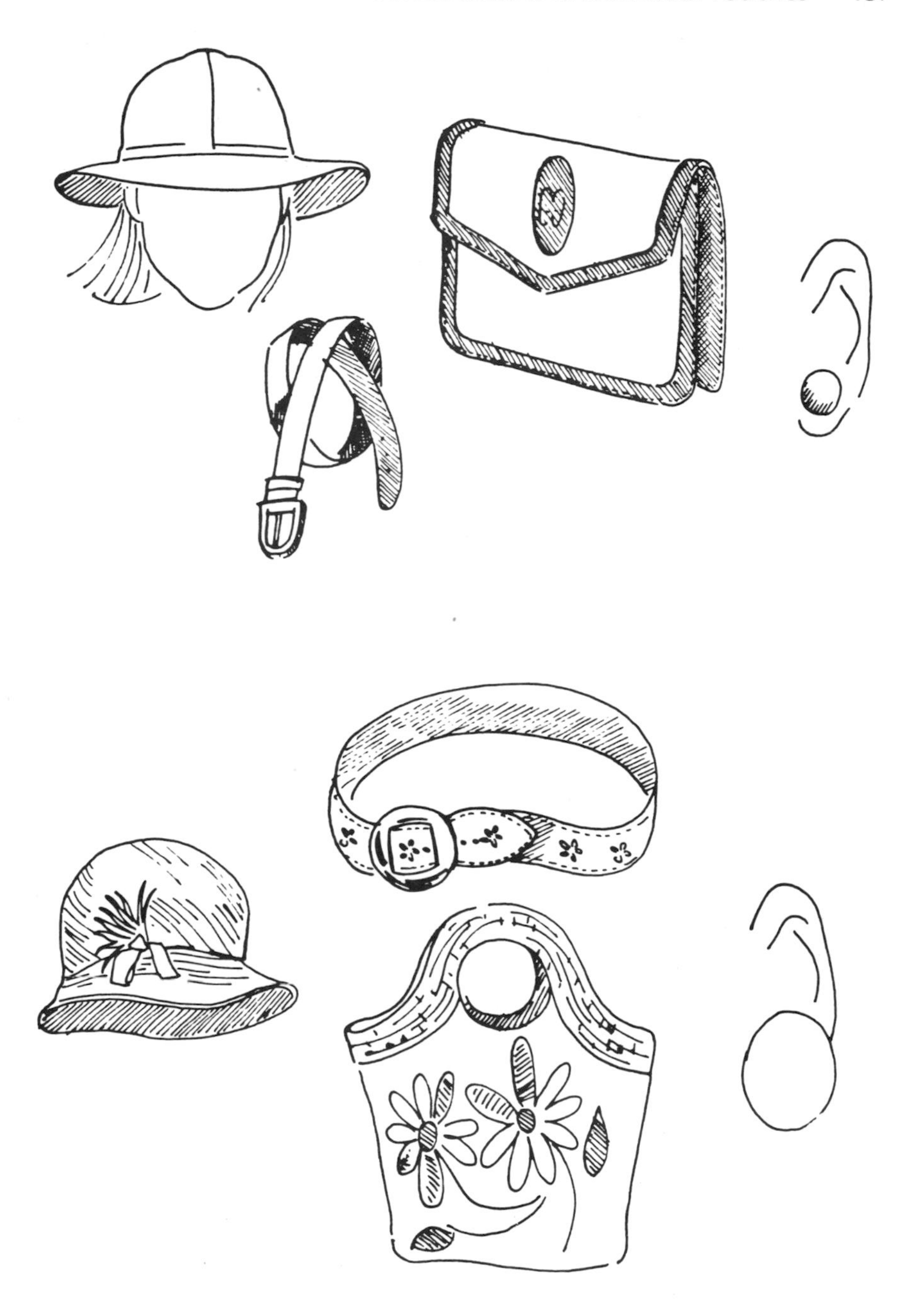

Accessories should be fun, but try to make interesting, not corny, selections. The above accessories show good taste, the ones combined below do not.

This combination mixes metals and contemporary designs with an antique design.

Enjoy the fun of your jewelry but remember to be interesting, not corny, in your selections. Your jewelry should reflect fine taste; avoid anything that gives a cheap connotation.

8

Special Wardrobes

There is something professional, competent-looking, and reassuring about a uniform.

If you take enough time to study the construction of a swimsuit, you will find that some styles are more flattering on your figure than others.

Fancy tennis panties, though cute, call attention to your bottom, so don't wear them unless you want to be noticed bottom first.

If you wear uniforms on the job, you may welcome not having to make a dress decision every day. You can dress quickly in preparation for the job and more thoroughly enjoy the remainder of your wardrobe when you are not working. And though you wear a uniform, you still want to look your best and feel feminine. A uniform is *your* uniform and should fit your body well and allow maximum comfort; no matter how much extra work it takes, have each one you wear altered to perfection. Whether your uniforms are one-piece or separates, they should look as though they were custom-made for you. Many large hotels, hospitals, and companies provide complete laundry and maintenance services for the upkeep of their employees' uniforms. If this applies to you, it can be a big advantage for your clothes budget and eliminate wear and tear on your personal wardrobe.

Though your uniform flexibility may be limited, some jobs allow for more individuality. If you work in a beauty salon, you may be able to wear pantsuit uniforms and colors. Stay away from white and select pastels instead. If an airline gives several uniform choices and you look best and work comfortably in pants, forget the dress option and wear pantsuits. Some jobs allow accessories; so try a variety of scarves and tasteful jewelry to eliminate the tedium of your uniform. If you are working in a hospital with children, if permissible add some objects of interest to your uniform: an eyecatching belt, bright-colored beads, or a sweater of multicolored yarn. If you are permitted style alternatives, think of a style that will be flattering on you. A tunic may be the choice for a longer, leaner look. A V neckline with short sleeves may enhance your neck, bust, and shoulders. If you are working in an outdoor beach or tropical atmosphere, an off-the-shoulder peasant blouse may be prettier than a scoop neckline. If shawls, caps, or vests are a part of your uniform, wear them in a way that strikes the right note for you.

There is something professional, competent-looking, and reassuring about a uniform. Even though uniforms limit your self-expression, and can become a bore when worn daily, a uniform stands for what you are doing and that in itself can be very individual.

Let's face it, too, not everyone wants to spend time each day coordinating, so a uniform can be of great help when you don't feel like getting it all together.

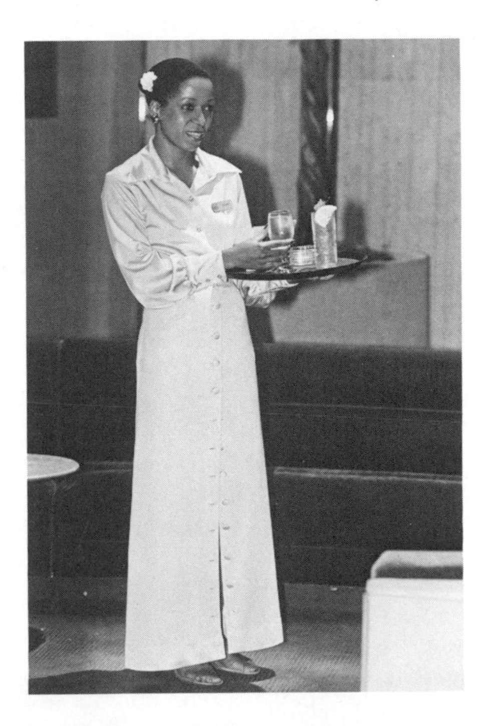

There is something professional, competent, and reassuring about a uniform.

Interviews with women who wear uniforms on the job indicate that their main concern is comfort. Fabrics that are hot become very uncomfortable when worn for many hours. Shoes must give the maximum support and comfort. Unstylish shoes are less noticeable when worn with a pantsuit than with a skirt. Even so, many women prefer the freedom of movement and the feminine feeling of being in a skirt or dress.

Women who work as cocktail waitresses say they prefer a uniform to have conversational interest rather than sexy connotations, something with an interesting fabric, or a skirt that is detailed. All of the women I spoke to were positive about wearing their names on a tag; they felt it enhanced their personal feelings about themselves and contributed positively to their contacts with their co-workers, customers, patrons, and others.

With a uniform, the make-up and hair require a lot of attention, so take some of the time you save by not choosing outfits and put it to looking your best in an understated way. Individualize from the chin up.

Your uniform should be in perfect order and speak well for the job you are doing.

Swimsuits: Dress and Distress

Only about one in twenty persons who attempt to lose weight actually succeeds over a long period of time. This is the reality. If you have unbulged yourself, enjoy it when choosing your swimsuit. Otherwise either accept your limitations or be one of millions who find it distressing to shop for a swimsuit. If you don't have the proportions deemed ideal by manufacturers, you will enter the fitting room with an armload of swimsuits, most of which are constructed exactly alike. Swimsuit manufacturers give us few style choices each season.

A swimsuit must be thought of as both an undergarment and an outer garment, designed to be appealing for sunbathing and swimming. There is little room for camouflage, but if you take enough time to study the construction of a swimsuit, you will find that some styles are more flattering for your figure than others.

Swimsuits are designed with the more youthful figure in mind, so if you are older and in good shape your possibilities are enlarged. If you have ideal measurements, you can choose between a constructed or an unconstructed style. The unconstructed suit gives shape to the figure through the use of fabric, the most popular combination today being a blend of Antron-Lycra and nylon. The fabric itself produces control of the bust, abdomen, and seat. Most women who are free of bumps and bulges will select a maillot (my-oh) style — a one-piece suit with a regular cut at the leg; or they may choose a one-piece suit, with the leg cut high up on the thigh, a two-piece suit, or a bikini.

Fit—front *and* rear—is important. The swimsuit on the left is too short, the length on the right is correct. A solid color would be even more slimming.

The woman with a more mature figure should look at other styles: a suit with a boy leg or an empire-style swim dress. The empire style has a high waist, short bodice, and loose skirt and is generally made in cotton or jersey. A one- or two-piece blouson style in a soft fabric is also flattering to the more mature figure; this style has become difficult to find, however.

Many suits for full-busted women are designed with bust cups. Some of these are rigid and don't give a soft look. An alternative is an underwire style. Underwires (or wonderwires) have become more popular in swimsuits of all styles and sizes, especially to give support and shape to the small bosom. Bust darts and shirring built into the underneath of the swimsuit also are designed to give shape to the bust. If you are large-busted be sure to buy a suit with ample room at the top; a top that is too small merely draws attention and makes you appear even larger. A bandeau bra or one of your own conventional bras can be worn under some suits for more support. The flatter-bosomed woman has more selections to choose from; she looks good in the slinky tank suit or soft bandeau bikini. If you do want to appear larger in the bosom, try these styles or wear a soft fiber-filled bra under your suit if it has

Mature figures can look good in swimsuits too. The fabric and styling should be soft.

a scoop or V neckline that will conceal the bra. The halter neckline is also good; it pulls the breasts slightly toward center, giving cleavage where perhaps none was before. Try a style that gathers at the bustline, too.

To give more length to the body, choose a one-piece suit with no belt. The higher the cut of the leg the longer the leg will look. Use color to establish proportion; to draw eyes up, wear a dark-colored suit with a light section at the top. For the leanest look, a solid dark color is best. If you should choose a stripe or pattern, make sure the design is not placed where you want minimal attention.

Whether you sun or swim, comfort is important. Straps, especially halters and crisscross straps, can be uncomfortable. When you are buying a suit,

Style should be flattering to your specific figure. These swimsuits are inappropriate . . . the women should be in one-piece, solid-color swimsuits.

move your arms, neck, and back to be sure the straps allow comfort. Be sure you have at least one really comfortable suit.

If you spend time near the water, you will want at least two or more swimsuits. The styles should vary unless you have discovered the perfect-fitting suit for your body. In this case, buy the same suit in two colors. If you sunbathe a lot, you may want variation between styles that are more covered up and those that are revealing. Swimsuits can be used to exercise in, but the suit must give good body support for this purpose. The suit should be made of a cool fabric to assure maximum comfort.

As with all clothes, good care leads to longer wear. Swimsuits take more abuse because they are continually exposed to sun, sand, salt, chlorinated water, and suntan lotions. Rotate the suits you wear to give the fabric time to air and regain its shape. All suits should be washed in cool water and mild soap after each wearing. Towel dry and hang or lay flat away from direct sunlight. Most suits pill (form tiny rough balls in the fabric) at the seat from contact with rough pool surfaces; this is difficult to prevent, though washing will sometimes smooth this area. With proper care a swimsuit can last three or four seasons. A well-made swimsuit may cost $22 and up. Because swimsuit styles vary only slightly each season, a suit on sale will not seem outdated the following season. Traditionally, swimsuits weren't put on sale until after the Fourth of July, but now many stores mark them down prior to the holiday. This is a good time to buy cover-ups too, choosing those that can coordinate with all of your suits.

If you buy a white or pastel suit, be sure to check the lining. These colors are transparent when wet and it is important that the suit be properly lined.

You can add new colors, prints, or stripes to your swim wardrobe and select various designs and fabrics, but in making selections remember the guiding principles: comfort, fit, and flattery for your specific figure. Take your time and have a knowledgeable salesperson assist you, since most swimsuits are not returnable. Almost all stores require that swimsuits be tried on over underwear, so keep in mind that the line you see when trying on the suit won't be there when your underwear is removed. Remember, too, to have your own bra sewn into the swimsuit for extra support or wear a bandeau style bra with your suit to give a little more bust control.

On the Green

Fabric is several strokes ahead of style. This is the unanimous opinion of golfers, professional instructors, and manufacturers of ladies golf clothes. Since so many people play golf in hot weather, their clothes must be as cool as possible. Skirts in lightweight cotton or blended fabrics are the first choice for playing comfort.

Many golf skirts are made with attached panties; the nylon ones are very hot but are easier to care for than the cotton ones, which are a bit cooler. Most women dislike the attached panty and will choose a style where they wear their own panty, but this style is not easy to find. Above-the-knee skirt length is the most graceful look and easiest to move and bend in. Some women prefer skirts that include a belt for tees to which they can attach a small zip pouch for balls. Others find belts too hot and restricting. Pockets are necessary, preferably in front so you don't have to reach into a back pocket. Other golfers favor golf shorts (not short shorts) or Bermuda-length shorts.

Your golf wardrobe should include at least three tops for every bottom. Women in the Northeast like the short-sleeved golf T-shirt, while in the South women tend to look for sleeveless T-shirts or cool tank tops. V necks and collarless tops are comfortable for hot weather too.

Colors vary from dark brown and navy to the softest pastels, the soft and lighter colors being cooler. Color-coordinate your golf wardrobe (see Chapter 6, "Planning a Wardrobe"). If you buy a complete golf outfit, think ahead as to whether the sweater or jacket can be enjoyed with other golf clothes too. Be sure your jacket is very roomy and has several pockets. Golf clothes that are too small will add to your handicap in a literal way.

If golf is your sport in cold weather too, add slacks to your golfing wardrobe. Knits allow more mobility than most other fabrics. Don't forget the need for pockets.

Insist on buying yourself a quality golf shoe. The shoe should be leather, which shapes to the foot and allows it to breathe. Synthetic substitutes are hot on the foot and will soon crack. You should have more than one pair of golf shoes so you can rotate them after each game. A quality pair of shoes will cost between $45 and $60. To coordinate with your golf clothes, some shoes are made with interchangeable tongues of different colors. If you take proper care of golf shoes they should last at least two years. When you are not wearing them, use shoe trees to keep them in shape. Shoes should be wiped off and polished after each wearing.

Some women wear gloves on both hands, but most wear only one. Be certain the gloves you buy are comfortable and give a good grip on the club. Though gloves aren't an expensive part of the game ($6 to $8), they are important. Dark colored gloves are more serviceable than light ones because the grip wears off onto the glove. Wash them in mild soap and water and lay them flat to dry. If you lay them flat after each wearing instead of crumpling them up into your golf bag they will retain their shape much longer.

The two most popular hat styles are the visor hat with an open crown, and the hat with a closed crown to shield both hair and face from the sun. Buy a hat that can be wiped off or washed.

Golf socks come in two weights, thin or thick. The thick ones will absorb more perspiration. Both come in assorted fashion colors.

Select a leather or vinyl golf bag; the cost will be in the $75 range. Be sure you purchase it from a reputable golf shop or store to assure good service if the bag should need repairs (straps and zippers do break). Your bag should have many pockets and compartments for golfing odds and ends.

If you travel to play golf, you want the maximum protection for your golfing paraphernalia. The new "airline" bag, which is smaller than the standard bag, has individual covers for your clubs and a hood to enclose the top of the bag. Canvas bag covers will provide bag and club protection. Be sure you have a luggage tag secured to your golf bag. Most of these travel bags have adequate room for your golf shoes too. A broomstick skirt (pleated to fold into the shape of a broomstick) will fit easily into your suitcase or golf bag. And don't leave your golf umbrella behind.

A Tennis Dress

When I began playing tennis my options were dresses, pants, shoes, and socks of white. But today the tennis fashion explosion is obvious almost everywhere, from department stores to the small shops that sell only tennis clothes. Colors vary from pastels to dark brown and navy, and styles include appliquéd dresses, nautical shorts, and warm-up suits, made of velour and velvet. British designer Ted Tinling believes that a bit of drama is required in tennis togs. His pettislips, worn under tennis skirts, may be lace or even orchid georgette. Red lace "fancy pants" and socks might be an advantage to your game.

Because there are so many tennis styles to choose from, decide which ones do the most for your figure. Separates will give you a wider range of outfits. If you pick a skirt, look at the rear view to make sure it is long enough and comes well below the crease between your seat and upper thigh. Shorts are attractive if you don't have a thick thigh. If your middle is thick, don't wear a fluffy skirt or a dress that has pleats. Instead pick a soft, simple style in a dark color, and be sure that whatever you wear is not too short. Fancy tennis panties, though cute, call attention to your bottom, so don't wear them unless you want to be noticed bottom first. Choose a plain untrimmed panty instead. There are also tennis panties made of control fabrics that give your seat and tummy extra support.

Tennis fabrics should be lightweight and airy enough to breathe, otherwise you will become too warm. Jersey, cotton blends, and nylon blends are coolest. Some of the polyester fabrics and knits are very warm. Halter necklines, turtlenecks, and off-the-shoulder styles usually are not comfortable for playing tennis. The coolest styles are scoops, those cut low, away from the neckline. If you have trouble with low necklines or sleeveless styles because your bra straps slip, you may use lingerie straps, which can be sewn

When choosing tennis clothes, consider what does the most for your figure. These separates give a positive look for her figure.

This is a positive back view. Make sure your tennis skirt comes below your seat and thigh for the most slimming effect.

Fancy tennis panties, though cute, call attention to your bottom. Don't wear them unless you want to be noticed bottom first.

into the garment, or wear a bra designed with straps that keep to your midline cleavage and neck rather than to the outside part of the shoulder.

Though white looks crisp and is cool, it is harder to maintain than most colors. Whether you machine- or hand-wash white, it eventually turns gray unlike pastel colors.

Today's warm-up suits are goodlooking off the court too. If you pick styles with jackets, you can coordinate the jackets with your other tennis separates. Don't pick fabrics so heavy they are cumbersome to play in. Your outfit should be roomy enough to allow additional layers underneath in very cold weather and to give your arms and legs proper playing room. Pull-on waistlines are best, otherwise you may have zipper or snap problems while you are moving about the court.

Tennis accessories include hats, sweatbands, racket covers, wristbands, fashion socks, and shoes. A properly fitting tennis shoe must be long enough to allow your toes to move forward when you slide on a clay court. Otherwise, you may injure your toes or toenails. Walk around in the shoe at home before you go on the court to make certain it is comfortable, heavy enough for support but not so heavy that it is awkward to move about in.

Looking good in tennis clothes is not the exclusive right of the young set.

The newer suede tennis shoes should be thought of as fashion sport shoes. Though they have the look of a tennis shoe, they are not the best shoe for playing tennis in because they are heavy on the foot and give little support. Most of the suedes are not washable. Both leather and suede tennis shoes are hotter on your feet than canvas shoes.

Tennis bags should be roomy enough to carry all of your equipment, including racket and balls. Choose a color and fabric that won't soil too quickly. The dark colors stay clean longer, and nylon can be wiped off. Some other fabrics are washable, including the linings.

Some women have taken up tennis at retirement age, instead of bridge or knitting. Cities are offering tennis lessons through adult enrichment programs, and private programs and clubs encourage tennis at any age. Looking good in tennis clothes is not the exclusive right of the young set. Dark pull-on pants with a pastel or bright-colored shirt, short-sleeved or long, will be appropriate dress on any tennis court. A sleeveless tunic vest or simple loose jacket will warm you up in cold weather.

A Jogging Tog

Morning, noon, and night someone in your neighborhood will be running or jogging. Especially in cold weather, experts suggest that your body be covered when you run to keep your muscles warm. Pick a fabric that absorbs perspiration. Cotton is best, or select velour, terry cloth, satin, or jersey with a cotton backing. Buy a size large enough to hang loosely. One of the newest styles has a drawstring at the ankle. Attached hoods are good for running in the rain or in a cold wind.

Running shorts are priced from $3 to $25. Shorts cut very high on the thigh or boxer style will be flattering if your thigh is heavy. The fabric you select should be either cotton or cotton-backed to absorb perspiration. Available colors can be almost anything — from vanilla and khaki to brights, lights, and very dark. Running styles can include shorts worn with T-shirts, tank tops or short-sleeved jackets. Short one-piece jumpsuits also are comfortable.

A good running shoe can cost between $25 and $35. It must fit well, which means having room enough at the toe. If you will be jogging away from home, a cotton drawstring bag will hold all of your needs, including a towel, headband, and your doctor's phone number. Joggers' pouches are available to carry necessary keys or change while running.

A Leotard and Tights

My exercise class has at least thirty women, from their early twenties to sixty, all actively engaged in self-improvement. We are there to work, and primping isn't part of the exercise. But I am amazed by the unkempt self-presentations some of these women make, as though exercise was not relevant to looking good.

Leotards traditionally have been worn by dancers, but now they are considered streetwear for going everywhere. They are seen at the most chic places worn with blue jeans under blouses, or topped by a dancer's type of flowing wrap skirt. Women are wearing them for exercising, sunbathing, skating, disco dancing, and entertaining. Some major designers have now added leotards to their couturier fashions to wear with silky skirts and pants at night.

The newest "everywhere" leotards (Milliskin) are made of Antron nylon and Lycra spandex. They have a shimmering look, can be used for swimming, and are sleek and clinging. Because they hug the body, no undergarments are necessary. But because the nylon Spandex material is so densely knitted, it is somewhat hotter to wear for vigorous workouts. The Milliskin leotards have new versatile shapes. If you want them for exercise be sure they are easy to move about in, otherwise save them for street wear. Depending upon your preference for bareness, you can choose from the high-cut, low-back halter, the racing-back tank, the almost bare maillot with crisscross spaghetti straps in the back, or the convertible, which can be worn strapless or as a halter. Cotton blends make up into comfortable leotards, and an abundance of styles and colors is available.

The traditional classic leotard remains the most comfortable for hard body work. It is made of nylon and is cool on the body. However, it is lightweight and for better body support you would do well to wear a bra underneath. Danskin, an established and well-known manufacturer of leotards and tights, makes an exercise bra of polyester, cotton, and Lycra spandex. This bra is without hooks or hardware for a smooth look under your leotard. If you wear your own bra, be sure of good support; the more narrow the straps the less likely they will show under cut-out styles. Traditional leotards come in many fashion colors. The best-known style is the scoop tank, and there are now many newer styles with both long and short sleeves. Because most leotards do not have a snap crotch, I have found the most convenient one to get in and out of is the zip front. There are many manufacturers and styles, and prices vary from $7 to $25. Leotards can be worn with the soft dancer's skirt which varies in price from $12 to $25, or the soft pull-on pants in matching or complementary colors.

Tights

Tights can serve a dual purpose in your wardrobe. Dance tights are available in most colors and come in several weights: professional weight (a closely woven knit), lightweight, and a heavier support weight. Most weights can be purchased in either seamed or seamless styles and with either the reinforced foot or the stirrup (open heel and toe) styles. The stirrup is ideal for exercising because the exposed part of the foot adheres to the floor or mat for better balance. The closed foot can be worn with your ready-to-wear. Most leotards are sized small, medium, or large. Tights are sized short or petite, average, medium tall, and tall.

To retain elasticity in both leotards and tights, wash them in cool water and mild soap by hand. Do not use a dryer because the heat will break down the elastic and rubber material in the waistband. Hang or lay flat to dry, away from direct heat or sunlight.

You will find many stores selling leg warmers and soft ballet slippers in white, pink, black, and iridescent colors and in soft dressy fabrics.

Dancers' togs are no longer worn only on stage and in class, but wherever you want to be cool, comfortable, and fashionably dressed at a reasonable price.

9

Logos, Labels, and Manufacturers

The best concept to follow in making costly investments is to select styles that will remain handsome for years.

As in other fields of art, some designers who are no longer alive remain influential, and their couture designs remain classics.

Many women insist on buying name-label clothing. Some of them do not feel secure in their dress unless a designer's name describes what they are wearing.

Yves St. Laurent believes "what's right in a dress is the woman who's wearing it." The value of a garment should be determined mostly by your own values. I recommend that you ask yourself, "Does what I am wearing make me feel and look good?" If it does, then regardless of price, your investment has paid off. The price is just one element in an expensive purchase; individual preference is another. It must be worthwhile for you, your feelings, and your lifestyle.

Labels and Cost

Suppose designer clothes make you feel better than clothes without prestige labels, but you are in a budget squeeze. Indeed, you may love the look and feel of a Chanel, a St. Laurent, or a Bill Blass but you can't afford any of them. Walking into a boutique or designer department only makes you depressed. What can you do?

You can summon up a slightly positive attitude and tell yourself you are walking into these stores for idea adaptations, that you will buy a copy with lines similiar to the original. Perhaps you are there to see what this season's fashionable colors are. Maybe you are there to buy a designer accessory which will give you flair or some sense of fashion security without making an unusually extravagant purchase.

You might go so far as to carefully select and buy one or two pieces of designer clothing, with the intention of wearing them over and over, using the principles of interchangeability and accessorizing that are discussed throughout this book. These fashion skills will permit you to develop a wide variety of looks with a very small number of designer pieces.

The best concept to follow in making costly investments is to select classic styles that will remain handsome for years. Wear updated accessories to prevent you and others from being bored or reminded that a particular blouse is several years old. Many garments made of fine fabrics never grow old but gain a finer look with age. Wool, leather, cashmere, and gabardine, if cared for properly, endure well.

Though you may not be aware of it, many of the women you admire in designer originals have purchased them in second-hand shops, or they are wearing a relative's or close friend's discards. Several years ago I was working in a thrift shop. Because I was there often, I knew which fashionable women were donating their clothes, and I knew their sizes. For $2 I bought a pair of French custom-made silk shoes that had been designed for a well-known Atlanta woman who wore them only once with a gown for her son's wedding. You may have to sift through racks of undesirables to delight in that one find. Discover which stores resell designer clothes. The clothes are often current in style and usually in excellent wearing condition. More and more fine antiques shops are selling antique clothing and unusual accessories too. These can include splendid handmade shawls, crystal beads, fine leather or embroidered purses, and lingerie of silk and satin.

Designer boutiques and department store designer shops welcome the sale shopper. A fine garment that originally was $250 can be marked down as low as $125 on sale. Larger stores may have several sales within the year, smaller stores sometimes more. Ask that your name be included on the "sale mailing list" of your favorite shops. Basic styles and fabrics may not be part of their sale merchandise, but current styles of the season will be. Wrap yourself in a Valentino coat without ruining your budget.

A Collection of Designers

What is couture (koo-*toor*)?

The terms couture and couture collection are used to denote fashionable, usually French, dressmaking or dressmaking houses. A couturier (koo-*toor*-ee-*ay*) is a fashion designer.

Couture collections include some New York Seventh Avenue designers. Couture clothes may begin at $2,500 and are custom made for an individual. Because of these extraordinary prices, few women can afford them. Valentino, Bill Blass, Yves St. Laurent, Marc Bohan for Dior, Halston, and Pauline Trigere are some of the few couture designers remaining. Their collections are pacesetters for fashion throughout the world. These designers are expected to use superb styling and natural fabrics, to introduce fashion ideas as many as five years in advance of a season, and to create fashion excitement throughout the industry. Some of their designs are originally presented as extreme, but are later modified to a more wearable silhouette after the initial impact of the season's "newest look" has been made on the industry and the public.

As in other fields of art, some designers who are no longer alive remain influential, and their couture designs remain classics. Younger designers who studied for years under their tutelage have now become prestigious under their own names. Marc Bohan studied with Dior, Givenchy with Balenciaga. Chanel designers have kept Gabrielle (Coco) Chanel's concept intact in their collections since her death in 1970. St. Laurent was Dior's foremost assistant, succeeding him as head of the House of Dior at the age of twenty-one.

Keeping Labels in Mind

Designer boutiques, a European concept, line the streets of Manhattan and are becoming the vogue in cities throughout the country. They carry couture-label clothes. American women are now accustomed to shopping in designer boutiques, both here and abroad. These boutiques may carry only boutique collections, with the prices beginning usually at about $250, or the collections plus ready-to-wear, the latter being less expensive. Many boutiques carry a designer's entire collection of boutique clothes, ready-to-wear, and accessories. Most boutique collections are designed by a member of a designer's staff and approved by the designer. The clothes are almost always made of natural fabrics.

A collection of ready-to-wear garments may or may not have the designer's artistic approval, but have been designed by his staff and have his commercial approval and label. The fabrics usually are natural, but may also be blended with synthetic fibers. Polyester may be blended with a natural fiber in its finest weave, but you will certainly never find double-knit polyester in a designer boutique.

Designer boutiques are proud of their fine merchandise. They give individual attention and employ fine dressmakers who are talented in altering to perfection, keeping the original lines foremost or custom fitting a specific style to your figure. Many boutiques do only hand sewing and make a point of not owning a sewing machine. If you would like a shawl in the fabric of your dress, they can have one made for you. If you wish an additional belt to wear with the same dress, one can be custom made. If you should buy, for example, a jacket in a classic design and fabric, two years later a classic pant can be bought to match. This would be impossible to do unless the garment was from a designer collection, since other ready-to-wear manufacturers cannot offer this. Many women are willing to make these investments because they are sure of fit, quality, and style and they want the designer label.

Getting in Line Behind Labels

Many women insist on buying name-label clothing. Some of them do not feel secure in their dress unless a designer's name describes what they are wearing. You have probably heard someone describe her new "gray tweed *Calvin Klein* slacks," or how a friend wore her "*Halston*" to dinner. Some women are disappointed if you don't ask the price of the item and will find a way to drop the $400 figure during the conversation.

Name-label dressing is on the decline for economic reasons: there are not enough customers who are able to afford the clothes, and many manufacturers of better merchandise have gone out of business. However, enough designer houses remain to satisfy the woman who is willing to pay. As noted above, a name label does not mean the named designer has actually designed the clothes. The original designer may no longer be living but the name remains, sometimes owned by a large company which may try to continue the workmanship and design ideas of the original designer. Don't buy a label because it is supposed to be fashionable. Have your own specific reasons for making these investments, if you do so at all.

Don't Dress to Impress

Anne Klein, Calvin Klein, Jerry Silverman, Kasper, and Mollie Parnis are some of the name ready-to-wear labels. These clothes are considered neither couture nor moderately priced garments, but fall into their own category of being individual, very fashionable, and not inexpensive. Don't buy these clothes for reasons of indulgence, but instead enjoy them for the distinct contribution they will make to your wardrobe, the way they will enhance your figure, and most importantly the positive feelings you will have about yourself when wearing them.

Buying Without Labels

Moderately priced merchandise is fine, if you carefully make your selections to achieve your own fashionable look. There is a knack to this. Here's how. If you buy a dress that has a belt in a matching fabric, don't wear that belt. Instead add a leather or suede belt (perhaps the designer belt you splurged on). The dress will now look different from others. If your blazer has very simple buttons, remove them and add a set of unusual ones. If you purchase a three-piece pantsuit, wear the coordinating blouse with other items in your wardrobe but a different one with the pantsuit.

These are some simple ways of individualizing clothes without excessive expense. Look at designer clothes and work out your own ideas. A new fashionable shoe added to your wardrobe can re-create your entire silhouette.

More and More Labels Mean Less and Less

Fads fade. For some years now logos, signatures, initials, names, and whatever else designers could dream up were stamped, stitched, engraved, embossed, and signed onto whatever they would adhere to. The idea was to promote the "symbol," regardless of how an item was made or what it was made of. Plastic purses covered with names and initials were selling for $150 and up. Polyester T-shirts with initials on bust lines, shoulders, and collars were being bought in rainbows of color for ridiculous prices. Initials were hanging from everywhere and anywhere in gold, silver, stone, and leather. Some women wanted the labels inside their clothes to be sewn instead on the outside. I hope that era has subsided and that women are more interested in stamping their clothes with their own individuality. It is more difficult to be your own trend setter, but it's certainly more appealing. Devote yourself to promoting *you* in your own personal way.

Designer Accessories

Don't make owning a designer label a goal to attain without a pertinent reason. I have enjoyed designer accessories for several reasons. Wallets, pouches, key chains, and other small items often are made in interesting patterns that will coordinate with any purse I carry. Dark shades will stay clean longer, and the patterns are inconspicuous enough to be carried with any clothes. Often I just need a little drop-in pouch for an evening bag, and will use the pouch that holds my make-up in daytime as my clutch at night. Some designer gloves, scarves, belts, watches, and hats have great flair. Choose these for their innovativeness, not to advertise someone's signature. Designer shoes and purses can be extraordinary in design or subtle. This shoe or that purse may launch your entire look. If a Charles Jourdan or Chanel shoe fits your budget and your foot, take pleasure in wearing it.

A Collection of Designers

These are some of today's name designers:

Adolfo came to the United States from Cuba and opened his own design house in 1962. He was originally well known for his Chanel-styled hand-knit suits selling for up to $775. He sees his Adolfo clothing as creating a feeling of comfort, elegance, and youth.

John Anthony, a New Yorker of Italian descent, says he designs for a small, strong audience. The lady must be slim and fairly tall and be able to pay $200 to $300 for a dress.

Geoffrey Beene, who lived much of his life in Louisiana, designs luxury clothes for up to $3,000 and has a Beene Bag collection ranging from $12 to $200. The comfortable, uncontrived look is what he stands for.

Bill Blass, Indiana-born, can sell you high fashion at $2,000 and Blassport styles for $25 to $350. His coordinated separates are worn by millions of American women.

Albert Capraro, Manhattan-born and originally an assistant to Oscar de la Renta, is a favorite of Betty Ford, Susan Ford, and Barbara Walters. Though he designs on Seventh Avenue, he sells to Middle America. His prices begin as low as $60. His styling is simple and wearable.

Diane von Furstenberg, born in Belgium, started by selling her clothes in America. She sold thousands of her soft wrap dresses, appealing to America's middle-class women. Her prices and styling tend to be moderate. Whatever she designs is manufactured by the hundreds.

Halston came to the fashion industry from Des Moines, Iowa. Believing that "less-is-more," he designs long, simple dresses in cashmere with matching sweaters, or little black dresses with imaginative necklines. He has become well known to lovers of Ultra Suede. His sportswear begins at $25, but you also can buy clothes at $1,000 in his collection.

Carol Horn likes to use innovative fabrics such as crinkled cotton. She emphasizes styles that look good anywhere, even lounging at home.

Calvin Klein's clothes are referred to familiarly as "Calvins" by their wearers. He is a most perceptive designer of clothes that are simple and uncluttered: a skirt, a cowled sweater topped with a jacket, a skinny coat.

Ralph Lauren, coming to the fashion industry from the Bronx, sees "his women" as American-looking girls who love the earthy, tweedy life. He emphasizes fine tailoring and simplicity.

Mary McFadden, from Long Island, studied design in Paris and prides herself on understanding and using exquisite fabrics. Working in Eastern silks, Japanese hand-painted batiks, Japanese pongee, and Indian tussah, she emphasizes soft, flowing dresses.

Oscar de la Renta, who has spent much of his life in Madrid, is known for extravagant styling, long gowns in particular. Fashion magazines rarely omit his name among important designers on the haute couture or high-style list.

Yves St. Laurent is considered by much of the fashion industry, worldwide, to be the most innovative designer alive. Unlike others, he has been able to bring a designer's influence to a mass market.

Jerry Silverman, a third-generation New Yorker, has for years offered the American woman clothes at affordable prices. Some Silvermans can still be purchased for under $200. His styling is feminine and he strongly believes in year round fabrics.

Valentino believes his clothes convey classic, understated elegance. Women who dress themselves in clothes by this well known designer are always cognizant of his excellent construction and beautiful fabrics.

Even though you may be unable to afford some of these designers' clothes, enjoy looking at them for the excitement and flair they bring to the world of fashion.

10

Travel: What to Pack . . . and How

Your trip's purpose and where you stay will make a big difference in how you pack.

When you travel, your clothes should be interchangeable.

There are many criteria to consider when choosing your luggage. Luggage should be considered part of your travel wardrobe.

Seasoned travelers must plan carefully to avoid packing too much, selecting the wrong clothes, and being burdened with overweight luggage.

The world is best seen with clothing and accessories kept to the necessary minimum. Many of us pack for a trip as if it were a safari with frequent dinner parties and no opportunity to buy anything more. When you finally get to wherever you're going, you usually realize that you can buy what was unexpectedly needed or inadvertently left behind. This chapter aims at finding the best compromises between taking your entire closet and leaving the basics behind.

Enough Is Probably Too Much

In support of the too-much and too-many traveler, it must be said that weather is unpredictable and you often need the same number of things whether you are away four days or two weeks. If you want to travel light, choose hot or cold and eliminate the in-between.

Your trip's purpose and where you stay will make a big difference in how you pack: working, sightseeing, entertaining, being entertained, visiting someone's home, or staying in a hotel. Your own personality is a factor. Are you organized, impulsive, impatient, a worrier, forgetful? Recognize your limitations and allow for them in applying the following principles.

Make Yourself Comfortable

Regardless of how you will be traveling, it is important that you travel in comfortable clothes. It is best to wear clothes that are neither too heavy nor too light. If you will be driving, you will want your arms free to move easily, so omit a heavy coat. Never wear boots when you travel a long distance, they are too confining to your legs and can prevent proper circulation. Instead wear a comfortable shoe. Soft slippers or slipper socks would be ideal to include in your purse or travel tote for assured comfort.

You will want to bring along a sweater in case there is too much air conditioning. Buses and planes are often chilly. A soft sweater you can fit into your tote will be easiest to manage.

A pair of loose pants will probably be the most comfortable to travel in for a long trip, since your legs will be covered in case of too much cool air. If you wear hose, they will bind your legs and become uncomfortable after many hours of sitting. Be sure that whatever you wear is not too heavy either. Bulky sweaters, turtlenecks, and heavy jackets can make you feel overheated.

For an enjoyable trip dress in comfort.

Carry Clothes That Work

The clothes you take should require as little maintenance as possible. You will try to minimize wrinkle and repair problems. Regardless of how short your trip is, many garments will need time to hang out or be pressed. Jersey, wool flannel, gabardine, knits, terrycloth, and many fabric blends are materials that wrinkle less than others.

Your clothes should be organized in plenty of time before your departure. Taking the time is a major fashion principle which I have stressed throughout. Usually you have one or two days' notice, often more than that. Don't take clothes that are not ready for wearing (buttons on, cleaned, properly hemmed), or clothes you have not first tried on at home. It is best to have worn the complete outfit before you take it away. Know whether the shoes are comfortable, whether the vest and blouse coordinate nicely, whether the pants fit you properly.

Some women buy a new outfit and never try it on again until they are far away. It can be very disappointing, to say the least, if you are not happy with something 500 miles from home. If you have the time and space, hang together all the clothes you plan to take, review your accessories, undergarments, and lingerie to be sure you are including all the things you will need. The easiest way to do this is to make a list, keeping in mind your schedule, the weather possibilities, and the extras you will need such as a hair blower, shampoo, suntan lotion, long slip, and bedroom slippers. It's easy to leave extras behind if you don't follow a check list.

If you will be visiting a place you have not traveled to before, get information about the climate, the type of clothes necessary, and the ease of finding what you may need while there. Travel bureaus, tour headquarters, chambers of commerce, airlines, and individual hotels may have this information for you. People you know may have excellent suggestions, especially if they have traveled to the same area. If you are taking a skiing holiday or going to a health spa, you may want to wait until you are there to purchase necessary specialized items to be sure you have the right things. However, if you do buy something at home, such as ski boots or an exercise leotard, keep the hang tags, sales slips, and other information just in case you need to return an item when you come back.

Is It a Plane, a Car, or a Bus?

Transportation makes a big difference in how you pack and what you take. Consolidation should be your goal. Do not pack to be away for months if your travel time is going to be much less, since nothing is more of a nuisance than being overloaded with luggage, garment bags, and an armload of boxes. Travel means your space is limited. If you can't carry your luggage yourself, you will be waiting for others to assist you. In airports, hotels, or even at someone's home, the extra hands won't be around when you need them. Limit what you take and know how to pack.

If you travel by car, you may have a little more room for those additions than when you fly or ride by bus or train. The airlines have become much stricter about hand luggage, so be sure to ask at check-in time what is permitted. On my last flight I was not allowed to go aboard with a large department store box, though I was not told this at the check-in counter. I took it on the plane, as I had done often in the past, but was told just prior to departure that it would have to be taken off and checked. After much negotiation with the stewardess, I was able to keep it on the plane, but I resented the airline's inconsistency and my inconvenience. Therefore, if you are carrying boxes or equipment, ask questions before you board.

Think Before You Pack: What Will I Need?

Eliminate the froufrou but not the enthusiasm. Your clothes should be interchangeable, which means you should carry mostly separates. If travel means work, leave your dressy things behind. Include a satin, silky, or chiffon blouse or a soft sweater for cocktail or dinner, since some evenings you may want to change from your work clothes. It is also important to include something very casual for after-business hours: a tour, an outdoor art show, or perhaps the zoo.

Even if your trip is brief, include an extra pair of shoes and hose and never forget your rain hat and umbrella. Remember a jacket, shawl, or sweater for cool weather or air conditioning, in a color which blends with all of your travel clothes. Pack a small purse if the one you carry for work is large and would be cumbersome at night.

What you wear to travel in should count as an outfit on the trip, too, and should be wrinkle resistant and comfortable. If you pack an extra blouse or sweater for this outfit you will have a fresh look to wear another time. I like to travel in and take clothes that are not my very best. Clothes get more easily soiled, damaged, or even lost during travels, so I leave my very favorites at home.

On business trips, the multiple-use and the accessory concepts should prevail. A belt that looks good at the waistline with your top tucked in should look good, too, over the same or another top worn on the outside. A soft silk carnation is colorful on a jacket lapel and eyecatching on a sheer shirtdress pinned at the waist, and it can change your hair at night if worn at the nape of your neck. If you are including a suit, wear it with a sweater or shirt by day, and fill the neckline of the jacket with pearls for dinner. A skirt or pants with a vest is one look, and the same top and bottom without the vest is another.

Putting the pieces together is like playing a game. Something new for you might be a very long tunic that you'd wear over a sweater and pants one day, then alone, sashed as a dress on another day.

There is an advantage to sleeves that can be buttoned at the wrist, or uncuffed and rolled on the next wearing. This concept works well with a blouse from last year of which you are tired: if you never wore the sleeves pushed up and cuffed, do so this year. This works best on blouses that don't have really full sleeves. Some cardigan sweaters will give you options too:

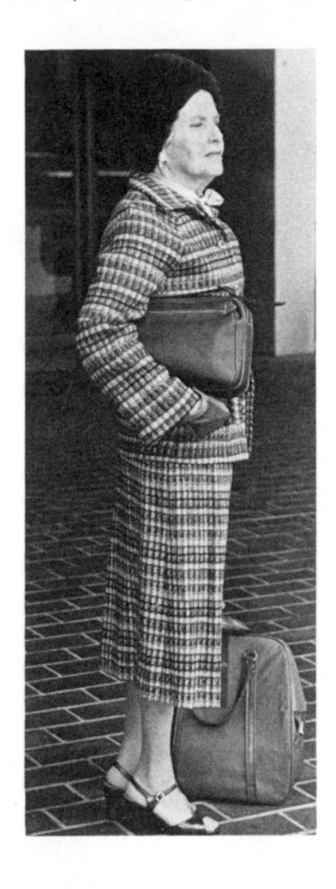

What you wear to travel in should count as an outfit on the trip too. Separates and accessories should have multiple uses.

Something new for you might be a long tunic over a sweater and pants. On another day wear it alone, sashed as a dress.

they can be worn around your shoulders on Monday, buttoned up on Tuesday.

On a long-awaited trip to the Bahamas, I kept spurring the jet on to assure myself time for sunbathing on the first afternoon. My luggage was eight hours slower, however, and I had no bathing suit or beachwear until it arrived. This taught me a packing lesson: if you want certain items upon arrival, such as swimwear, a tape recorder, ski boots, or change of clothes for a meeting, take them on the plane with you. And it's good insurance to carry your toothbrush, make-up, and medicine. Anything especially vital or valuable, such as jewelry, business papers, or car keys, should stay right with you.

Sun and Sand

Off to the beach? Will you be staying in a cozy informal cottage, or sunning at an island hotel? These are two different trips and your beach clothes will differ accordingly.

If your vacation is casual, than take casual clothes. There is no need to pack a long dress if your activities will not call for evening wear. For the more casual trip, you will need at least two or three bathing suits so that one is always dry. They should differ in style if your aim is allover suntan. Suits that are elaborate in design, with crisscross straps or cut-out peep holes, leave unattractive tan marks. For classical sunbathing, your suit should be simple and have straps that can be removed or hidden for sunning. Two cover-ups should be included, one long and the other short. The long one is to protect you from the sun and cover your entire body.

A short cover-up or pair of beach shorts can go over your suit for relaxing away from the water. If you can find a short or long style that will double as a robe you will eliminate an extra piece of lingerie. Caftans in jersey, jumpsuits in terrycloth or velour, or drawstring shorts and pants are excellent for the beach. Whatever you take along must be washable.

Pack two pair of beach shoes, which can double as slippers, since you may walk a good bit on or to the beach. Be sure they are comfortable and stay on your feet well. At least one pair should be washable. Lots of scarves and a straw sun hat shouldn't be forgotten, and your own beach towels could be important for seaside relaxing. Nights often are cool, so take a sweater, light jacket, or shawl that also will be attractive when you are not at the beach. Wear your shawl with your swimsuit too. In addition to shorts, slacks, and tops, include a sundress and a skirt. There are days you may want to go into town, shop, or eat out and you will enjoy a change of clothes.

Remember the beach extras: two pair of sunglasses (one pair may be lost or broken), a bathing cap for the pool, suntan lotion, a sun-screen lotion for protection, and aspirin in case you get too much sun too fast. A beachbag is a must, and plastic-lined ones are best. Make it large enough for your various necessities, which might include a thermos and a "bug off" spray.

Hotel Sun, Hotel Fun

A resort hotel calls for a goodlooking beach wardrobe. Whether your stay will be a few days, a week, or longer, it will take time for you to get it all together. You can be smashing without extravagance.

Take along three or more swimsuits for sunning and swimming. Alternate them to allow time for each to dry and air. Your cover-ups, one long and one short, should be pretty and coordinate with your suits. These cover-ups may also be necessary off the beach, since some hotel lobbies and restaurants require that your suit be totally covered. Huge scarves and shawls are great to look at and can conceal well, though they may not meet some restaurant requirements. If you can't find the size of scarf or shawl you want, make your own. Choose a fabric you like and cut it into a large square or triangle; hem the edges or leave them sheared. Also use the shawl around your shoulders at night. Remember to pick a color or pattern that will complement your other clothes. Terrycloth or jersey pants, or long or short skirts are easy to jump into at the beach; use your swimsuit as a top or add a zip jacket, shirt, or pullover to be more covered. These bottoms can double as streetwear too.

If you want to look your thinnest, your swimsuit should be a dark color, either solid or trimmed in a contrasting color. If your thighs are not your best feature, make sure the trim is not around the leg. Patterns and stripes are fun, but look at yourself from all angles to judge whether the stripes call attention to the wrong places. Put the pattern strength into your cover-ups if you look best in a solid-color suit (see Chapter 8, "Special Wardrobes").

Two pair of beach shoes should be sufficient. The higher the heel the thinner your leg will look. If the color is neutral it will blend with all of your beachwear. Interesting beach styles come in straw, clear plastic, canvas, and leather. If you like to sand-stroll, do it in a shoe that can be wiped off or washed.

Your entire time will not be spent in the sun. You will also be shopping, sightseeing, lunching in town, and in the evening there will be dinner, dancing, nightclubs, and parties. Don't pack on impulse. Take time to be sensible with imagination and flair and to create a mini wardrobe that will stretch. If you have been more basic in style and color with your at-home wardrobe and you want to buy a few extras for vacation and resort wear, take a plunge with more dramatic colors and styles. Choose either brights or lights on top or bottom; white is super with dark skin or a tan. If white pants aren't flattering, consider a white linen jacket or eyelet shirt.

Take along a mix of color in shirts and T-shirts . If you select styles with scoop or V necklines, they will be right for nighttime too. Try for blended fabrics or synthetics that are washable and have the look of pure fabrics. Don't forget the gauzy and filmy cottons. Mix, don't match, your bottoms. Include pants and skirts, at least two in soft fabrics (jersey, cotton gauze, silk blend, cotton voile) in styles appropriate for evening wear as well. A long skirt or patio dress is a good resort item if it includes a shawl or jacket, since the shawl or jacket can change the look of your outfit for another night and also can be worn with the other clothes you take. One pair of shoes may be enough; if your beach shoes are also pretty with your clothes then another sandal with a higher heel may be all you need. A daytime casual purse and one small evening bag will do to carry small things. Some of the new cosmetic bags in prints and stripes are grand and not expensive; many are priced under $10. Use one either day or night for that extra purse.

At a resort hotel you may tend toward a too-extensive wardrobe in an effort to show variety to the other guests. But you want to avoid having a lot to pack and unpack. The solution: put your accessories to work. If you bring along two or three silk flowers they can be worn one night in your hair and another time pinned at the waist. Be daring and experimental with your other accessories. Satin cord belts can be tied around your hair. Shawls can be tied as fanny wraps. Huge colorful earrings will light up your face. Scarves, lots of ribbons, and little hats (turbans and print skull caps) will hide your hairdo imperfections, and somehow on holiday they look just right.

For completeness, pack a plastic-lined beach bag, a straw beach hat, bathing cap, two pair of sunglasses, lotions and creams, and a mild detergent to wash out swimsuits and lingerie. If you tan, you may need darker make-up. Sunburn may cause your undergarments to be very uncomfortable, so take along loose panties and a very comfortable bra just in case. At least one of your nightgowns should not be too bare, since hotel air conditioning can be chilly. You aren't on a deserted beach, and most resort areas will have attractive shops for any other items you may need, so have fun shopping.

From Your House to Their House

Although you may want to remain forever, don't let it show. Closet and drawer space is often limited, so bring along your own. I never travel anywhere without my hanging lingerie bag. Until recently these bags were hard to find, but now most luggage shops, department stores, specialty shops, even bed and bath boutiques have them. A hanging lingerie bag is a soft fabric bag that has many different sized zippered pockets. Each compartment can hold small items such as underwear, hose, scarves, gloves, folded nightgowns,

Experiment with your accessories when you're away. Satin cord belts tied around your hair, flowers, and little hats somehow can look just right.

costume jewelry, belts, etc. A nice feature is a pouch for soiled laundry that extends the width of the bag. Lingerie bags can be folded in your suitcase and later put into a drawer, or they can be hung in a garment bag and then in a closet. They eliminate the scattering of small items within your luggage and save you time unpacking and repacking.

Include a robe that is comfortable for lounging, but not a see-through. Add a very revealing robe if you are going to visit him, or else wear his.

If you are visiting for a specific occasion, this may call for special items. You will probably do well to ask your host or hostess in advance of anything in particular you may need. If you are visiting during a rainy season, you will want your raincoat, umbrella, and rain hat. If the weather will be very cold and your coat isn't heavy, include sweaters to wear underneath.

When you are entertained at someone's home as a guest, you would like to strike the proper balance between overdressing and dressing too casually, since you are trying to fit in with their milieu and their expectations. Why not ask and discuss the possibilities before you arrive? In a home with children, when you plan to spend time playing with them, take along some things to wear that are not your very best. My mother always packs a couple of cool, comfortable changes for on-the-floor and backyard playing (since grandmothers really like to play). You might be seduced into finger painting for the first time in thirty years, or trying your skill at soccer. As I have repeated elsewhere, foot comfort and shoe changes are often neglected. As a house guest, one day might be lunch, another a family picnic, and at night dancing. So a mild shoe fetish is okay.

The Key to the City

Which city, what time of year, and what is your schedule? My own travel experience has convinced me that most cities are the same. You will do a lot of sightseeing, roam in and out of stores, eat too much, and share time with friends. If the weather is hot your day will begin unpleasantly, and remain so, unless you are dressed especially to be cool and comfortable. Cold days will freeze your activities if you are not especially careful about your warmth.

A good friend from New York recently visited Atlanta where the temperature was sweltering every day. She was saved by her straw hat. Take a hat, especially if you are not accustomed to very hot weather. Make it lightweight and comfortable and wear it a lot. If the hat is a natural straw, you can vary it each day by adding scarves, ribbons, feathers, or flowers to the crown or brim.

The fabrics you wear in hot weather should be as light as possible: seersucker, gauze, cotton blends, cotton challis, frail silks, soft denim, sheer crepe, soft synthetic blends. Polyester is acceptable only if it is combined with another fabric or unless it has been processed for a quality look. Pure polyester clothes are much too hot and they don't look good. In very hot weather skirts tend to be cooler than pants, which stick to your body and wrinkle. A style that is full or softly pleated is best for coolness. In addition to short sleeves, the less fabric on the neckline and shoulders the better. Consider tops of filmy cotton or gauzy and stringy fabrics with low scoop or V necklines, and narrow straps. Stay away from turtlenecks and cowls on very hot days.

There is great variety in separates, but with the right use of accessories you will get much versatility from dresses too. A dress with a jacket or cardigan sweater can be a champion. A natural, nubby cotton or slubbed linen dress will take you from day into night. Wear it shopping with the jacket, minus the jacket for dancing. An Indian-motif shawl can top most of your clothes, and a shawl will keep you a little more covered when you need to be.

Pins, earrings, bracelets, and other jewelry pieces are important to change your dress expression. Keep yourself in the travel spirit with layers, belts, vests, and at least a couple of purses — a roomy one for day and something small but functional for night.

Though city life is more casual today than it was in the past, it is still wise to have at least one outfit that is a little dressier for dinner, dancing, or partying. A short dinner dress will take you anywhere, unless you have been advised to have something long for a convention dinner, benefit party, or company function. Contemporary dinner dresses are available in linen, matte jersey, sheer cotton, challis, wool flannel, or crepe. They can have an interesting vest or jacket, or be in styles that can be worn with a silky blouse underneath.

Lots of shoes are a must since your feet will be used and abused. Big cities demand walking. Despite autos, buses and subways, if you want to see a city you must walk. On a long day in town, a shoe tote can be worth its weight by enabling you to switch shoes midday or evening. Shoe totes come in many fabrics and designs and can hold one or two pair. Pick the lighter weight, and before you buy it try it with your own shoes inside. A nylon or canvas shopping bag is convenient for dropping your shopping purchases into, and it can be carried on the plane too.

If the weather is cold, keep warm with a wool muffler, gloves or mittens, and a coat with a hood. Particularly if you walk in snow, a hood will cover your hair and be warm around your ears and neck. If your head, ears, hands, and feet are bundled up your entire body will stay much warmer. Layers of clothes create air spaces that keep in heat. Opaque tights, heavy knee socks, and boots are good for warmth, and sweaters and heavy vests will shield you from chilling winds when a coat just isn't enough. Come to the city and come prepared.

Destination Europe

The following advice should be applicable to most European holidays. Because of the strict airplane luggage weight allowances, you must condense your wardrobe. Wintertime or cold climates mean heavier clothes and more cumbersome luggage. A city requires city clothes. European casual clothes are a bit different from the down-home look. You will need more skirts and dresses than pants because in many European cities pants are frowned upon. If you choose skirts and dresses you won't be faced with the question of what is appropriate. But if the weather is severely cold, you will want at least two pair of heavy pants for the days when you walk a great deal and sightsee. Pants are worn much less frequently at night in Europe, so you might dispense with dressy pants entirely.

For winter months a velvet blazer can enhance a daytime or nighttime outfit. During the day you can accessorize the blazer with a striped wool scarf under the jacket collar, worn with a wool sweater and corduroy skirt, and cover your head with a knitted cap. At night the same jacket and skirt would be perfect worn with a soft shirt and patterned scarf. If you have worn boots during the day or a sporty walking shoe (be absolutely sure to take along a sturdy, comfortable walking shoe), switch to a pretty pump at night. If you go to a private party or dine at a fine restaurant, one long dress or long skirt in an easy-care fabric (jersey, knit, Qiana, or a washable crepe blend) will be formal enough, and either short or long will take you to almost any European disco or nightclub. Knits for day or evening are easy to accessorize and care for too.

Because many European cities have a rainy season, you should take a raincoat. Choose between one with a heavy zip-out lining which can also serve as a winter coat, and a plastic, nylon, or vinyl lightweight raincoat that will be full enough to wear over a heavy coat. Some of the newer styles are long capes or ponchos, and some fold into their own pouch. These are also serviceable if the weather is warm. Some of the newest vinyl, tissue nylon, and plastic styles are colorful and attractive and very different from the clear plastic and almost ugly look of the past. You will need a rain hat and umbrella too. Carry a fold-up umbrella in your purse.

One knit suit that is wrinkle free will be a standby as you travel from country to country, and you can change your sweater or blouse often to feel as though you are wearing something new. Pick a suit style that can be belted or unbelted, worn with a vest and without, layered and easily accented with scarves, shawls, and jewelry. A large shawl or scarf that covers the head is often appropriate for entering European churches.

You will feel much more comfortable in strange lands if your style of dress is fairly conservative. It is not necessarily wrong to be different, or even to stick out as a tourist, but I would rather you did this by choice. If that is your choice, then I recommend learning what the local customs and attitudes are and discovering whether you like the new possibilities of self-expression. European theater, ballet, and opera encourage chic clothes but not flamboyant dress.

Your lingerie and undergarments should be easy to maintain while you are away. A soft, comfortable robe will be great for relaxing in your room, and a pair of slipper socks or soft foldable slippers will help reduce the hotel-room chill.

Try to tuck in the following extras when you pack. A smaller purse than the one you travel with and carry during the day. A wool muffler and mittens or gloves. As many pairs of shoes as you can take, because you will be doing a tremendous amount of walking and your feet will require TLC. Jewelry pieces are easy to tuck into suitcase corners or jewelry rolls, but costly pieces should either be left at home or be kept in the purse you carry with you.

If you will be away for two or three weeks, the following should stretch for your stay: one suit, three skirts (or one dress and two skirts), one jacket or blazer, one or two pairs of pants, six to eight tops, and one dressy outfit. For additional time away, make top and bottom additions.

Beyond metropolitan Europe you may travel to the seaside, to quaint villages, to someone's home, or to lush wine country, and you will need a change from your city clothes.

Seaside, the atmosphere is casual, and you will feel most comfortable in informal clothes. Concentrate on fabrics that are easily packed, wrinkle free, and washable. In addition to the separates, the long dress or skirt you wore in the city will do well at a beach resort, worn with a shawl instead of a jacket. If you are in a more lavish atmosphere, include one or two more-dressy outfits.

If you make short side trips in Europe, have at least one or two skirts or pants that will be easy to drive or travel in.

Luggage and Lots of Other Things for Travel

A bag is only as good as its performance, and comedian Alan King has fun with this cliché when he finds his very expensive luggage at airport baggage claim. One piece is ripped, another has a broken zipper, and another a damaged handle. He is further affronted by a simple cardboard box tied with string resting there in perfect condition. He will not give in . . . he will continue to use expensive luggage, but now he will protect it in string-tied cardboard boxes!!

His saga rings true. Luggage gets damaged regardless of its price. Never-

You are seen with your luggage. There is a vast selection of styles, fabrics, colors, prices, durability, and brands to choose from.

theless there are many criteria I want to discuss in helping you decide what to buy. Luggage should be considered part of your travel wardrobe, so its appearance is significant. You are seen with your luggage. It also holds your wardrobe and therefore its functional ability is extremely important. There is a vast selection of styles, fabrics, colors, prices, and degrees of durability. The first questions to ask yourself are: How many pieces do I need right now? What price range can I consider? Which styles and functions will best accommodate me on the usual trip? A person who flies a lot has different problems than the person who travels primarily by car, bus, or train.

GARMENT BAGS

A slim-line garment bag has three hangers and carries about six pieces of clothing. Larger garment bags will carry twelve to twenty-four garments. There is also a jumbo garment bag which is made of three detachable units; it is virtually a closet on wheels, since typically it comes with wheels attached.

Most garment bags are made of various grades of nylon, canvas, or duck cloth. Pick one of high-grade material rather than one so lightweight or flimsy that it will tear or rip easily. The framed garment bag is sturdier, but it can be heavier to carry than an unframed style.

Most recent styles can be carried unfolded or folded. If you carry it unfolded and hang it, be sure it comes with a strap or cinch to keep the hangers from slipping down and that there is enough room to fit the hangers easily into the bag. It is also extremely desirable to have a handle or strap on the bag for carrying and hanging instead of having to use the hangers themselves for this purpose. If you will be carrying it folded be sure the handle is sturdy and comfortable for carrying the bag like a suitcase. Removable pouches or pockets on the outside of the bag will allow you additional packing space when you need it. If your garment bag does not come with hangers included, use strong metal or wooden ones, not standard wire hangers since these bend easily.

If you haven't used a garment bag before, you will enjoy the ease of staying partially packed when traveling. Your clothes will already be on hangers. You can pack the bag easily by laying it on your bed or by hanging it on a sturdy hook over the door. Layer your clothes on each hanger, beginning with pants or skirts folded over the crossbar. Use a piece of packing tissue to cushion the hangers and between layers, or pin your skirts and pants from the waist onto the hanger. Next add your heaviest clothes. The last clothes on top should be the lighter weight or crushable fabrics. Though you don't want to make the hangers too full, you should be able to fit several pieces on in layers. I have found the best way to prevent wrinkling is to encase each fully clothed hanger in a plastic bag, such as those you save from the cleaners; keep them in your garment bag to reuse each time you pack. When you get to your destination you can immediately remove the hangers and hang them in the closet. If your garment bag is deep, your hanging lingerie bag will fit in too.

LUGGAGE SPECIFICS

Standard luggage usually comes in these different sizes: 26 inches (regular), 24 inches (the weekender), and 21 inches (the overnighter). Additional pieces are a tote, which is a large soft bag, and a make-up case, which is small and rigid.

There are three basic luggage styles. Molded luggage is made of a hard substance on all sides. Semisoft has a frame which closes with a locking lid. Soft-sided luggage is made from a fabric that will expand and usually closes with a zipper; some pieces are framed and others are not.

Molded or semisoft luggage should lock securely with either a key or combination lock. If with a key, carry two sets of keys; if with a combination don't forget the number. My husband selected our anniversary date for his combination, forgot what he selected, then remembered it was our anniversary and forgot the date. Don't take chances; your birthday might be all you can remember. This luggage often weighs more than soft-sided luggage and is not expandable. A hard blow may make a dent or hole in the luggage, but if you carry any breakables (and you really shouldn't) they are more protected than in soft luggage.

Soft-sided luggage is usually lighter in weight. Because it closes with a zipper, you must know the limitations of zippers. Don't put too much pressure on them. When closing this luggage put your finger under the zipper all the way around as you zip to be sure that materials, plastic bags, or tissue paper do not get into the teeth. Soft-sided luggage will expand, giving you more room to fill the corners, or squeeze in an extra piece on top. Remember that all luggage should be packed full. If you have excess room fill it with tissue, not newspaper since the print may come off on your clothes. Although overpacking is the culprit behind many broken zippers, don't underpack either. The aim is to equalize the pressure throughout the case to avoid tension and hold your clothes as securely as possible. Soft-sided luggage has some resiliency and will bounce back if subjected to a hard blow. If the fabric is heavy and of good quality, tears and holes will be less likely.

Quality luggage should last at least ten years with normal wear and tear; inexpensive luggage will have to be replaced much more frequently. Remember that luggage is for protection. Three hundred dollars worth of clothing may require more than a forty-dollar suitcase. It is not necessary to buy the most costly luggage, but whatever you choose should be made well, both in its material and construction.

Luggage should make a statement about you or indicate a psychological preference. It should make you feel good when you carry it. The next time you visit an airport or hotel, watch what people carry. Many will pack in cardboard boxes, paper or plastic shopping bags, or outdated, damaged, or soiled luggage. Women who are well dressed want a fashion look in luggage too. Colors may include earth tones, browns, black, khaki, navy, burgundy, dark red, tweeds, or chic patterns.

Luggage materials include molded plastic, leather, vinyl, canvas, corduroy, nylon woven fabrics in needlepoint or tapestry, or a combination of materials. Canvas and nylon are two fabrics that are not very costly but have a modern and attractive look. As I have said several times and will say once more, select a good quality, not the $10.98 version that may not even last

The next time you visit an airport or hotel, watch what people carry.

one trip. If your travel is limited, buy only one piece of luggage but make it something that will last indefinitely.

Ballistic nylon is popular, reasonably priced, and durable. Du Pont has introduced a nylon fiber, Cordura, that is being used in soft-sided luggage because it is strong, lightweight, attractive, and fast-drying.

Many clothes designers have lent their names, logos, and patterns to today's luggage. The look is handsome, the price is expensive, and the durability is no greater than for other fine luggage. The designer usually has nothing to do with the construction; you are paying for his or her name. If you like the look, if the construction meets your approval, and if you can afford it, buy it. The best-known designer luggage bears names like Yves St. Laurent (YSL), Pierre Cardin, Halston, Diane von Furstenberg, and Charles Jourdan.

Your luggage should be considered part of your wardrobe. If you travel for business, it should have the same quality look as what you wear. If you choose leather luggage, you are buying quality and looks but the cost is high. Canvas, corduroy, and other fabrics cost less. The style and color should convey the look you want. You will want your luggage to last a long time, so take time in making your selections.

WHERE TO BUY LUGGAGE AND WHAT QUESTIONS TO ASK

Luggage is sold in luggage shops and luggage departments in larger stores. As with other expensive items, and because of various wear-and-tear hazards, buy luggage from a reputable retailer who will stand behind his merchandise. Luggage shops usually have a larger assortment as well as salespeople who are qualified to give specialized information. If you buy your luggage wholesale or discounted, you may not be able to return it, replace it if damaged, or add a matching piece at a later date.

The most important question to ask the retailer is whether the luggage you have chosen is available as "open stock." This means you can replace it or add other matching pieces later on. If you go to a reputable store for a well-known brand in a pattern that has been in the line for several years, you are increasing the probability that the same style and pattern will still be available ten years from now. Your luggage can also be repaired more easily and quickly if the parts (zippers, locks, etc.) are readily available from the manufacturer. Parts from less popular brands and styles often are discontinued.

Beware of luggage on sale, since it is often a discontinued style or something that has been made specially for the sale promotion. You are safest with standard manufacturers, styles, and colors. You are not safe with fad items, unless you want a piece of luggage for a specific need or look and don't plan to add to it; then a novelty piece can be an excellent addition.

A number of conveniences have appeared on the market to assist you in transporting luggage.

MORE LUGGAGE SPECIFICS

If you travel frequently, the strength of your much abused luggage is vital. It will be easier to carry if the handles are comfortable and padded. Some styles have one handle, others two. Luggage with two handles should be carried by both since otherwise you will put too much pressure on one handle and cause it to rip or break. Some small pieces of luggage have handles as well as a strap, which allows you the option of carrying it over your shoulder when you need both hands free.

If your storage space is limited, either at home or at your destination, it is important that your suitcases can be condensed as much as possible. Many styles permit several pieces to be stored one inside another. Some soft pieces can be folded and stored in their own pouch or in a drawer. Some framed styles have removable frames for storage convenience.

A number of conveniences have appeared on the market to aid you in transporting luggage. Some luggage pieces come with attached wheels that can be stored underneath the case or removed when you are not rolling. Other wheels are more permanent and cannot be hidden. Luggage with wheels can be pulled by straps or handles that conveniently disappear when not in use. Do-it-yourself buckled bands with wheels can be strapped around a piece of luggage for pulling it along. Rolling carts are available in chrome finish or other metal for carrying one, two, or three pieces of luggage. Be sure to buy a sturdy cart that folds small when not in use. A good one will cost you about $25.

Security flaps come attached to some luggage, or straps can be purchased separately which fit over the zipper or lock for extra security should either break.

Interior restraining straps are a feature to consider, especially if you frequently go through customs or security. These are attached to the inside of the suitcase and help to keep your clothes in place when the luggage is inspected. I have not found them useful for a large piece of luggage that is packed full, since they are not usually long enough to go around deeply stacked clothes.

Always label each piece of luggage with your name and address. This is required by commercial airlines. Luggage tags come in various styles and prices; attach them securely to all luggage, regardless of your mode of transportation. Include these tags on cameras, typewriters, attaché cases, calculators, or whatever will be important to identify. The labels should include your name, address, and phone numbers — home and business. In addition to the labels or tags attached to the outside of luggage, a label should be included inside with the same information plus your travel itinerary, indicating how, when, and where you can be reached.

Because your luggage often is similar to other travelers' luggage, it is wise to make it easily identifiable. It is always possible that the label may get lost and you will have to describe your luggage. Embossed initials or a small chain hanging from the handle can be a big help in these situations.

INNOVATIVE PIECES

If your travel is brief, or is water or sports oriented, a duffle bag is ideal. Most of these are made of waterproof canvas, duck, or nylon. Varying sizes and a multitude of colors and patterns are available. Because they are soft they can be stuffed full. Pockets and zipper pouches give more room for odds and ends. Most duffle bags have comfortable handles as well as shoulder straps for easy carrying. The insides may either be entirely waterproof or have a waterproof section to separate your wet and dry clothing. Since they are easy to fold, you can pack duffle bags in your other luggage for later use. A good quality bag is safe enough to go overseas, and if skiing is your sport the expandability will allow for the bulky garb you will take with you.

Leather duffles are soft and supple. Consider one of these for weekends away or as an airplane carry-on. For a personal touch, have your initials or name printed on your duffles.

There are also soft packable travel totes which expand from small to medium or large. When not in use, they hide away in their own storage pouch. Most totes can be carried in your hand or over your shoulder. They make weekend trips by car or air easier and can be filled with personal items for safe carrying right along with you. I use mine as a travel purse and find it equally important when I travel by car and require only a few items for a one-night stay. This saves unpacking a large piece of luggage. The more pockets and pouches the better for keeping little items such as keys or tickets within easy reach.

If you decide on a separate case for your make-up, breakables, toiletries, and medication, get one that is strong enough to protect what is inside and roomy enough for all you wish to include. Some cases have removable trays to use as shelves, since motel and hotel rooms never seem to have enough bathroom shelf space for items you want at hand. Don't pick a bulky make-up case with wasted space. The best linings are those you can wipe out with a damp cloth. You want to be sure you have room for larger items such as shampoo, hairblower, etc. The items that may spill should be enclosed in plastic zip pouches. Many of the harder cases can be checked through as airline baggage.

What You Should Know About Airlines

Air travel regulations differ from one airline to another. Domestic and international travel regulations change frequently. For the most up-to-date airline information write to the Civil Aeronautics Board, Washington, DC 20428, and ask for their airlines rules and regulations pamphlet.

You can no longer carry your favorite piece of hand luggage or decorative store box down the jet aisle. Carry-on bags now must not exceed 30 inches in largest measurement, and the bag must fit under your seat. If you carry an overlarge tote, you may be stuck with it in your lap for the flight, unless you are lucky enough to find the seat next to you unoccupied and have room enough to store it underneath that seat.

Know the airlines' procedures in plenty of time before you depart. Check your luggage at least twenty minutes before domestic flight departures, and forty-five minutes before international flights. Stay by the side of the skycap or ticket agent as airline luggage tags are affixed to your luggage to be certain that you and your luggage arrive at the same destination.

Most of the damage done to baggage at airports occurs when bags are caught in conveyor belts, thrown on top of other luggage, or placed near grease. Regardless of the price of your luggage, it can get damaged. Airlines do not give tender loving care. In case damage occurs, be sure you keep your airline ticket and go to the proper authority. If it is very late at night and no one is on duty, call early the next morning and have your ticket for verification. Most major airlines will take responsibility for repairing, cleaning, and replacing any luggage that is damaged beyond normal wear and tear. Be assertive. You are the customer, you support their service, and you have many rights.

A Knack to Packing

Packing is not simple and there are many alternative strategies. My best advice is to experiment with different methods, because each trip is different and each piece of luggage functions differently. Nevertheless, I do have some suggestions for packing a suitcase.

First get together all the items you are taking with you. Then make sure they are in good wearing order. Next, fasten all zippers and buttons and remove hard belts. Now start by putting the heaviest items (e.g., a book, large purse, portfolio, radio, or electric rollers) along the bottom of the case. Think about placing clothes in layers and in sections. If you do not take a garment bag you will have more pieces of clothing to pack in your suitcase. To prevent wrinkling and to cut down on bulk, pack in sections, grouping similar items in the same areas rather than randomly. In one section place clothes lengthwise, respecting natural creases. Begin with the longest items, such as pants. In another section fold the next longest items, such as skirts, placing the waistbands at right angles to prevent bulking. You can either use the clothes themselves as layers or place tissue or lightweight plastic bags between the garments. Try packing a fragile item inside a plastic bag; expel the air from the bag or it will take up too much room. Fragile bows, necklines, and sleeves should be covered with tissue to keep their shape. Lightweight items, such as nightgowns or robes, should go on top. If your coat is very bulky, wear it or carry it in a garment bag over your arm.

Shoes should be placed in shoe mittens and filled with soft things, such as socks, a soft belt, or coin purse. If you are packing in soft-sided luggage, pack shoes and other heavy items opposite the handle; with molded luggage, place shoes near the hinge.

Your purses should be protected with purse covers or wrapped in a scarf or tissue. Remove all hard objects from the purses, since they will leave a mark. Handles or chains should be wrapped. If you don't have a lingerie bag, fill purses with stockings or a slip to keep the purse in shape and save space. Belts can fit around the edges of the case. Fill luggage pockets and pouches with items such as bathing suits, a soft hat, or an umbrella. Be sure any items with hard edges or points are protected.

Put what you will need in a hurry on top. Distribute weight evenly and pack full enough, with clothes and tissue, to keep items in place. Don't overdo it, since luggage under stress does not hold up well.

Remember not to close your suitcase until the last minute, even if you have finished packing the night before your departure. It's a good idea to wait until just before you leave to pack those garments that wrinkle or crush quickly. When you arrive at your destination, open the suitcase immediately to reduce pressure on the contents. The quicker you remove your clothes from the suitcase, the more time they will have to hang out. You will find, if there are wrinkles, that some of the wrinkles will fall out naturally in just an hour or two. However, if wrinkles persist, use your hand steamer or hang your clothes carefully in the bathroom and rely on the steam from the shower to smooth out remaining wrinkles.

Here are some specialized items or extras that can make going places easier, more convenient, and much more pleasant.

A coffee kit. Available in a small canvas zip bag. Includes either a small coffee pot or a hot-water immerser, two mugs, plastic spoons, and containers for coffee or tea and powdered cream.

Alarm clocks. Available in several different travel styles. See whether it ticks too loudly, in case you prefer quiet.

Large bar of soap. Most hotels and motels have very small bars. Take yours in a plastic soap dish.

Ear plugs. If noises disturb your sleep. Hotels and motels are not as quiet as home.

Night light. To see in an unfamiliar room.

Steamer. Never leave this behind. The small hand steamers are easy to pack, and wrinkles will disappear in moments.

Skirt hangers. Tuck a few in your suitcase for skirts and pants.
Lingerie hangers or clothes pins. Ideal for all of your washable lingerie, and will assure quick drying.
Needle and thread. A sewing kit can prevent panic. Take a few safety pins too.
Spot remover. Available in individual pads, which eliminate the possibility of spilling in your luggage.
Polish remover. In individual pads, to eliminate spillage.
Folding umbrella. To keep in your suitcase when traveling, and in your purse or attaché otherwise.
Folding tote bag or collapsible case. Folded in your luggage when departing and filled with purchases or extras when returning.
Extra watch and eye glasses. Always be prepared.
Electric rollers and hair blower. Both available in travel size for more compact packing.
Lingerie bag. More of a necessity than an extra. Individual pockets store underwear, costume jewelry, scarves, belts, etc. Eliminates packing these by the piece. You never need to unpack them either, since this bag will hang in a closet or fold in a drawer upon arrival. It should include a pouch for soiled laundry.
Travel mirror. Excellent for quick make-up application at home, office, and on the road. Choose one that has a magnifying mirror on one side and a regular mirror on the other. A gooseneck rod makes the light adjustable. Some can be hung around your neck to keep your hands free. Attractive carrying cases usually are included.
Plastic bottles, jars, and soap dish. No need to travel with large breakable bottles. Fill plastic ones with the make-up and toiletries you will need while away. Small cases of plastic or leather include their own small bottles to hold pill and vitamin needs. Mark each bottle to avoid medical errors.
Molded plastic covers. Safe and sanitary protection for razors and toothbrushes. Or, you may prefer the throw-away toothbrush and razor instead.
Make-up bags. Come in many sizes and shapes. They should be plastic lined. Those with individual sections or pockets are best for separating small items (shower cap, nail polish, toiletries, shampoo, etc.).
Adaptors. Often needed overseas for electrical plug-ins.
Cotton shoe mittens. To keep shoes unscuffed, unscratched, and clean. Most come in a package of three or four pair.
Jewelry roll for your purse. Keeps your jewels protected and separated by the piece. Something easily broken (a watch) should be packed alone.
Luggage cleaner. Some luggage can be washed or wiped off. Other fabrics should be sprayed with a special water and dirt repellent. Spray when your luggage is new and again periodically. Most luggage or notion departments have this spray available. Wipe off your luggage after each use to keep it

clean. If it is leather use a clear paste wax several times a year to keep the leather conditioned.

The more you travel and experiment with various methods and accoutrements, the easier getting ready to go will become.

The Store

11

Preparing to Shop

Don't shop when you are rushed and don't shop when you are tired.

You know your wardrobe and your needs better than a shopping companion. Don't rely on other people to make your dress choices.

Develop a shopping plan. Think about what you want to buy on a specific shopping trip, and decide which stores have the most promising selections.

Preparation is necessary if you want shopping to be a satisfying experience. Shopping well is a complex skill that requires planning and alertness. Don't shop when you are rushed and don't shop when you are tired. Successful shoppers are those who know how to be comfortable and avoid stress and fatigue. Sometimes you will make a favorable purchase on impulse, but this is usually one item, and a very different matter from coordinating many things in your wardrobe. When you are fatigued, you don't feel or look your best. Clearly it's not a good time to shop.

How to Find the Time

For women who live and work away from both the city and the suburbs, access to stores is obviously limited. Shopping is a problem also for women with very little spare time. Catalogue and newspaper shopping can often be the answer to these shopping dilemmas.

How do you handle those items that come in different sizes? You can try telephoning before ordering to find out more pertinent size information. If the store or catalogue source is out of town, writing may be cheaper than phoning. Ask if the item is cut true to size. If they tell you that it is cut on a smaller scale, then order a size larger than you usually wear. Make certain that whatever you choose can be returned if the fit is wrong or you don't like the item.

Fortunately for those with limited free time, many stores throughout the country offer evening shopping hours; some shopping centers stay open as late as 9:30 P.M., including weekends. More recently, stores have been offering Sunday shopping hours, usually after noon.

It will be less tiring and more productive if you don't shop on a day you've spent working. Choose instead an evening or weekend when you have not worked. If you work evenings, visit stores in the morning, but try to avoid a rushed feeling and give yourself ample time between shopping and beginning your work day. Have an exact idea of what you are looking for. Have a shopping list.

If you are shopping to learn what is available and to sharpen your ideas, you may want to spend an hour or two looking in several stores and at assorted merchandise. In this situation, don't plan to buy that day but return a day or two later to make your purchases.

If you believe that you never have any free time for shopping, I suggest keeping a schedule or log of your week. Then make whatever hard choices are necessary. How important is it for me to shop? What must I give up to get time for shopping? When can I do it most conveniently?

Dress for Shopping Success

Success at shopping requires that you dress properly for it. It is ludicrous to see women, straight off the tennis courts, still sweating, dashing into stores looking for cocktail clothes. How would you ever get a clear picture of yourself in crepe de chine while wearing a tennis cap, wristband, and tennis shoes?

Here are some ways to prepare yourself for a shopping trip:

Your make-up and hair should have a finished look. But don't come straight from under the dryer if you are going to be concerned about messing up your hair.

Wear undergarments that are appropriate for the clothes you are looking for. You may have to bring several bras, slips, and pantyhose with you. Sometimes you will have to borrow them from the store while you are trying clothes on.

Bring more than one pair of shoes with you, since different lengths require different heel heights. This is especially true if alterations are required.

Always shop in clothes that are easy for you to get in and out of. You may be taking your clothes off a number of times, and difficult zippers, buttons, or too many layers of clothes will be a burden.

If you are shopping for something specific, such as a top to go with pants or shoes to go with a dress, bring the other item with you. It is difficult to match colors, fabrics, and styles when you are guessing by memory. What looks right in the store may be a poor match when you get it home.

If you are looking for something you have seen advertised, bring along the ad to help the salesperson find what you are looking for quickly.

Try not to shop right after eating, when your figure is filled out. If you have edema or swelling during your period, this too is the wrong time to try on clothes.

Carry all of your packages in one sturdy shopping bag. This way you won't lose small bags, and it saves confusion too.

Shopping Is a Private Affair

Browsing or window shopping is a time to share. Real shopping is best done alone. I recall my mother telling me about her frequent shopping experiences with her best friend. Mother is tall and attractive with lots of flair, and her friend short and overweight. My mother realized that what she was buying for herself was all wrong since she was relying on her friend's input and taste.

Don't rely on other people to make your dress choices for you. You know your wardrobe and your needs better than a shopping companion. Shopping should not be a family affair or a matter for relatives. You don't require the approval of mother, daughter, or husband. If you can't do without a little support, first narrow the choices to two things you like. Then ask, "Which of these two looks better on me?"

Sometimes you may need guidance for a particular reason, as when you are going to a city you have never visited and need to know what is appropriate for the climate. You may be unfamiliar with the dress conventions for a wedding service. There is a difference between asking for advice and letting another person decide for you.

At first you may find it difficult to shop alone, but stick with it until you become comfortable.

Why Overspend Your Energy?

Many women persist in shopping all over town, which adds confusion and usually is not necessary. By limiting your shopping to three stores, you get to know the merchandise and the salespeople, and you can feel confident that they know you. If the stores have a wide assortment of merchandise and prices are not too restrictive, there will be all the variety you need to complete your wardrobe. I have favorite stores both at home and away. I like some for sportswear, others for dressier clothes, and two in particular for shoes. There will be times when you shop in a new store for a different look, or in a store that specializes in a specific item you may want (a fur jacket, tennis clothes, silk flowers). Each season you might try a store you haven't been in for a long time. The three-store limit is not an absolute. But when you are coordinating a specific look, concentrate on shopping in a few stores. Running from mall to mall usually is wasted energy, and you become too confused to buy anything.

La Liste

After you have planned your wardrobe for the season (see Chapter 6, "Planning a Wardrobe"), make short lists of the things you will be shopping for first. Bring these with you on a planned shopping day and keep them with you in case you have time for an impromptu purchase. The best way to make a list is to categorize potential purchases into ready-to-wear, undergarments, accessories, replacements. I suggest buying ready-to-wear first, then undergarments and accessories. Or else work on clothes you are adding to or replacing, such as a cream silk blouse or black suede shoes.

People often make the mistake of buying their accessories first and then looking for something to wear with them. This is a strategic mistake and is impractical too. For example, when buying shoes, the color, style, and heel height may be wrong for the outfit you buy later. If you shop in the wrong order, you will exhaust yourself looking for clothes to match your accessories.

Develop a shopping plan. Think about what you want to buy on a specific trip, and decide which stores have the most promising selections. If you are looking for beachwear, shop in the store that concentrates on beachwear. Dress accordingly, since you would not want to wear boots, hose, and cumbersome undergarments on a day when you are looking for a bathing suit.

If you are shopping out of town, which is often the most fun time to shop, remember to keep all the pertinent information about your purchases, especially if you are having them mailed home. Keep the salescheck, the name and address of the store, and the name of the salesperson. If they have a mailing list ask to be included, since you might enjoy catalogue shopping at a later date. I have favorite stores out of the city and write them for special purchases such as a brand of make-up I have found only in their shop, or slippers I would like to order in an extra color, or handmade jewelry they carry exclusively. I keep my shopping information catalogued. It may be a year or two before it's time to reorder an item, but I will have the store, name, brand, and size written down. If you rely on labels, after a time they either fall off or fade and become illegible.

What Time Is the Right Time?

Do you sometimes shop for shoes at the end of the day, when your feet are swollen or tired? If you buy them early in the day, the fit will be more accurate (though you should try them on again in the evening at home to make sure they are still comfortable).

I advise my clients to stop shopping after three hours, before fatigue and frustration set in, and particularly if they haven't found what they were looking for. Concentration and decision-making ability deteriorate with too much shopping. There is definitely a point of saturation. Your results also will be better if you shop early in the season to prevent a last-minute rush for something to wear that night. Plan to shop for a vacation ahead of time. I don't believe that shopping quickly or under pressure results in good decisions.

Comparison Shopping

Don't overcompare. I know women who will use two tanks of gas, two days time, and their last bit of energy to compare prices. If you are just browsing, though, it's a good idea to look at price tags. It will familiarize you with the current season's prices, the cost of certain brands, and the price differences from one to another store. I have seen a two-dollar price difference on identical dresses in stores across the street from each other. One may be a specialty store and the other a department store that can afford to offer the dress at a lower mark-up.

If you are looking for a red T-shirt, a novelty belt, or a white lace blouse that won't get a lot of hard wear, you should look at several in different stores and compare the merchandise and the prices. This is a good time to pay less, if the look is right.

Bringing Them Home

There is no need to have clothes wrinkle before you wear them. The best way to prevent this is to ask the store to use a lot of tissue if your purchase is foldable. If it can be hung, ask that they put it on a hanger in a plastic bag. You can hang it in your closet until you are ready to try it on again. Most stores will be glad to do this if you ask, since carrying a hanging bag with their name is good advertising.

Remember to be prepared, based on the above recommendations.

12

Shopping Methods for Various Types of Stores

If you want a positive outcome from shopping, you must practice and learn to shop skillfully.

There are four different categories of stores: department stores, specialty stores, boutiques, and discount operations.

Have you ever shopped in Penny's, K-Mart, or Lerner's? These stores often have some of the latest fashion trends at very low prices.

Do you know how to shop? I have spent years as a personal shopper and have collected data from friends, salespeople, and my family. I am convinced that many people don't know how to shop. When people say they don't like to shop, the truth usually is that they haven't yet learned the necessary skill. Because we have less time for shopping and because so many stores compete for our attention, shopping is becoming a lost art and a source of confusion for many. If you want a positive outcome, as you would in tennis, piano, or skating, you must practice and learn to shop skillfully.

Get to Know Your Stores

In many cities it is impossible to shop in every store, although most of us think we are missing something if we don't cover them all. The truth is that you can coordinate your wardrobe better if you use fewer stores.

There are four different categories of stores: department stores, specialty stores, boutiques, and discount operations. A *department store* carries the broadest assortment of merchandise, including men's, women's, and children's apparel, shoes, accessories, home furnishings, and hard goods. The price structure usually includes both budget prices and costly specialty merchandise. A *specialty store* sells selected lines of merchandise. The variety is more limited than a department store's, and the price structure is narrower and usually somewhat higher. A *boutique* is a small store selling ready-to-wear and accessories. The merchandise is usually fashion oriented, eclectic, higher priced, and very specialized. *Bargain operations* — discount stores, outlets, and sample shops — are all similar in that they emphasize low prices, few amenities, payment by cash or credit card, and almost always a no-return policy.

Every store has a feeling or atmosphere that the customer senses. Stores can be friendly or unfriendly, up-to-date or behind the times, well organized or unorganized. Whether you feel welcome and at ease in a store has a lot to do with the attitude of the salespeople. The general tone of a store is set by the decor, the merchandise and its arrangement, the displays, and such extras as flowers, plants, music, and even perfumed air. The customer who feels at ease in an elegant and very fashionable store may not feel comfortable in a store that is only adequately decorated and carries no fashion merchandise. The reverse is also true.

Snob Appeal

Stores may try to appeal to certain kinds of customers, but their main interest is still in selling merchandise. A friend of mine owns a boutique in an exclusive shopping center and prides herself on appealing to a certain clientele. She makes little effort to pursue customers who aren't fashion oriented, but she still wonders why some potential customers are afraid of her store's image. She recently told me about shopping with her daughter in a new discount store and feeling very out of place. She was dressed in expensive, high-style clothes while the other customers were unstylishly dressed. She was uncomfortable and finally realized that her own store would have the same effect on people who had not shopped in an expensive boutique.

In a department store, the price structure is varied and a wide assortment of merchandise is available.

In a boutique, the merchandise is usually fashion oriented, eclectic, and specialized.

You have a choice of where to shop. If some stores are not within your budget, you may still have enough self-confidence to browse.

The Right Store for You

My husband usually finds shopping unpleasant and disorienting, since he doesn't know his way around stores and tends to be overwhelmed. Be aware of your own limitations and discomforts and make allowances for yourself. If crowds make you uncomfortable, shop in small stores. If you react negatively to "community" fitting rooms, large discount stores are not for you.

In planning to shop, decide the type of store you want and the various clothes you will need. As when buying in a grocery store, it is much better to have a list or at least a plan.

There are many other factors besides the merchandise that will dictate your choice of store. If you are in a hurry you might select a small store where you get personal attention quickly. If you have more time and price is important to you, you could select a discount store. I generally prefer a small store, although some of these don't carry a full range of accessories, coats, raincoats, or other items I may need, so I must also shop in department stores for those things.

How to Survive Department Stores

When I shop in a department store for the first time, I keep wishing I had a map. It's hard not to get lost, particularly in the older downtown department stores. In front of the long line waiting for the elevator is a directory with departments listed in either small or hard-to-read lettering. If you can peer over the heads and read it before the elevator comes, you can decide which floor you want. First time around, I usually fail.

It is easy to become confused by the many different departments scattered throughout the various floors. If I am coordinating an outfit, the job becomes more difficult. However, by asking I often find that a salesperson will assist me with merchandise from other departments. Be persistent, and explain that you would rather try on all the merchandise in one fitting room.

In an unfamiliar store, be sure you take the time to browse in each clothing department or you may miss finding what you want. Department stores usually have their merchandise arranged by categories: sportswear, daytime wear, evening wear and cocktail clothes, shoes, handbags, accessories, lingerie, coats, and rainwear. There are now more and more boutiques within department stores, and the big stores take a lot of time to cover. You will find a skirt and jacket in one department but the blouse in another.

There are many pluses to shopping in department stores. Various customer accommodation services are available, including delivery and lay-a-way plans. The price structure is more varied than in smaller stores and you have a wider choice of payment methods. Also, department stores run more sales and special purchases than smaller stores, and carry the more familiar brand names.

To make department store shopping more pleasant, try to select a salesperson who can help you each time you shop. Don't shop at the busiest hours, such as lunchtime or Saturdays, and shop when you have plenty of time.

What Makes It Special?

There are two kinds of specialty stores. One kind carries almost exclusively a single type of merchandise, such as jewelry, shoes, handbags, or jeans. The other kind is a specialty store such as Neiman-Marcus, or Lord and Taylor. These stores carry a broad assortment of merchandise but are more limited than true department stores. Their prices may not always be extravagant, but the range of prices is narrower and less flexible than in a department store.

Specialty stores with more moderate prices have opened throughout the country in the last several years. Examples are Ann Taylor, Lilli Rubin, Ups and Downs, and the older Casual Corner. These stores usually stress current fashion trends and have depth in the items they specialize in. Some specialty stores carry many import fashions. Some cater to a younger clientele and others to the thirty-and-over woman. If you are not of the young set but want blue jeans, don't be afraid to shop in a store that promotes them, since your selection will be much broader.

In some specialty stores you will be able to dress yourself from the inside out. Lingerie, accessories, coats, and raincoats will be sold. If the store has a good sales staff, you can sometimes enjoy more personalized service than in a department store. If you shop in the store often, they will make efforts to special order something for you or call you when a particular garment comes into the store. Some of the older well-known specialty stores pride themselves on the unique services they provide. Coffee or wine is served in your fitting room, where a single alterations expert attends to all the clothes you have selected. Department stores have these frills too, but less routinely. For the store to offer such services, you are charged within the cost of the merchandise. If the prestige and convenience are important to you, then you will enjoy shopping in a specialty store.

Clutter, Clutter, and More Clutter

When I first shop in a boutique, I'm never sure what is being sold and what is part of the decor. Once I went into a shop to buy a dress and came home with a lamp. Regardless of how funky or how elegant a boutique may be, there is something in every corner. The store is eclectic, which is part of its positive appeal. Boutiques are confusing because the merchandise is scattered throughout. At the same time, boutiques are exciting because, as with an attic, you're never sure what you will discover in each nook or cranny.

Many boutiques concentrate on exclusive merchandise, often one-of-a-kind items, assuring you an original look. But often just the dress you like is in the wrong size. You can enjoy the fun of the latest fashion looks, but ask for assistance so you won't miss what you're looking for. The right salesperson is most important in helping you coordinate your look. She — or he — will show you the newest way to wear the newest fashions, which is not easy even for experts.

European and designer boutiques are opening all over the country. Names include Halston, Yves St. Laurent, Pappagallo, and Givenchy. The prices are high, but if you have a favorite designer you will get the best selection of his or her styles. Other stores will carry these designer names too, but with fewer choices.

A Bargain Is a Bargain Is a Bargain

Don't be a grabber when you shop in a bargain store. Of all the stores you will shop in, this kind requires the best eye, the most time, and the truest shopping skill. A bargain is a bargain only if your purchase is right, since the biggest waste of money is to be stuck with something you will never wear. Price can be enticing, but know what you are paying for.

Ask yourself two questions when you shop in a bargain store: 1) Is the item something I really need? 2) Is the price low enough that I can buy and enjoy something frivolous that I would not have otherwise? If either of these can be answered in the affirmative, then you may not go home sorry.

You must take time to check out discount merchandise. Does it have flaws? Does it fit properly? Will it last as long as you want it to? Is the garment clean? Are its design details — pockets, buttons, etc. — intact?

Most bargain stores get their merchandise from a variety of sources, and the labels usually are cut out of the garments. Some clothes are overruns (the manufacturer cut too many), some are samples used in showrooms. Others are irregular because of improper sizing. And some merchandise is definitely damaged. Many of these stores sell for cash only and have a no-return policy, so you must be more than usually careful about your choice.

Since the merchandise here may be last season's, you are safer when buying a basic style, such as a blazer, terrycloth cover-up, or a pair of gabardine pants. The danger zones are passé styles such as outdated culottes, a hem length much too short, or a cape that is not relevant to your wardrobe. When I shop in these stores, I get the most satisfaction from a novelty item such as a satin multicolored jacket, which I would only buy because it's not costly. My thinking is that if I wear it only a few times I have still gotten my money's worth.

Most discount stores offer minimal amenities. The fitting room may be one large room. Merchandise may be crammed together on the racks or stacked on tables. Alterations and delivery are not available, nor are salespeople either in some cases.

Training Yourself Into Shape for the Label Fight

Some very well-known stores offer "labels" at bargain prices. If you arrive there early in the morning, usually midweek, you can watch ringside as ladies fight over labels. The stores advertise, "Buy from us and save dollars." You will, but your shopping skills must be well developed.

The best approach to this type of shopping is to do roadwork in other stores first, looking at the designer clothes and knowing the prices. Then go back to the discount store bargains. If you get lucky you might find the exact thing you are looking for, but more often than not in the wrong size. To take full advantage of this situation you must return to these stores routinely and keep alert, realizing that luck is involved. If you have the time and labels are important, why not?

A well-known store offers line-for-line copies of many designer clothes, which it shows to affluent and fashionable women at its own fashion shows. If you are there, you might just be lucky enough to buy a $600 copy of a $1,500 original.

Why These Stores?

I often talk to people about where they shop and why. People commonly say "I like the merchandise," "I like the location," "I feel comfortable shopping there," or "The salespeople are helpful." Some people tell you they only shop in the most fashionable stores; others talk about bargains. Some are reluctant to say they shop in stores known for less expensive merchandise. Regardless of your clothes budget there are good reasons to shop in, or at least be familiar with, all types of stores. The most interesting wardrobe should incorporate various price ranges. In my lectures and classes I have worked with merchandise without price tags to teach people to differentiate among variously priced items.

Surprising Sources

Have you ever shopped in Penney's, K-Mart, or Lerner's? These stores often have some of the latest fashion trends at low prices. There are certain items of dress for which quality isn't the issue, but the right touch is. I am referring to things like knee socks, summer straw belts, cotton print turbans, clear lucite earrings, and cotton beach bags. For these purchases, a higher price tag does not denote "better."

But if you are looking, for a durable and goodlooking briefcase, then shop at a store that emphasizes quality leather for this item. You will find a better range of briefcases, and possibly some things well worth your investment, though you wouldn't think of buying your entire wardrobe there. This concept is difficult for people with few shopping skills. Your choice of store is the result of an interplay of many factors, including cost, style, suitability, and various personal considerations.

I especially suggest shopping in more expensive stores during their sales. At least twice a year most stores throughout the country offer their merchandise at sale prices. This is a wise time to buy basic items that you will wear a lot, such as a coat, jacket, basic pants, raincoat, or flannel skirt. These stores have quality garments that wear well. Even if the price is more than you would ordinarily spend, this could still be the most economical choice.

If you are looking for a special garment for a special occasion, such as a wedding or a party you are giving, look to these stores.

Have you shopped in Tiffany's, Mark Cross, or Charles Jourdan? Though these names convey only expensive prices to some people, they also have items that are not prohibitively expensive. Tiffany's carries a fine assortment of silver jewelry pieces under $50. The silver Mark Cross felt-tip pen for about $35 may be a worthwhile purchase for you, and Charles Jourdan has some shoe styles you can find nowhere else.

Do Dollars Make the Difference?

Whether you spend a lot of money or little money on your wardrobe, you must establish your own personal image. Many stores, much time, and certain skills go into assembling a wardrobe. Being so prestige-conscious that you will shop only in prestige stores will be limiting to your wardrobe and to your shopping skills and confidence. There are clothes and accessories I enjoy wearing and feel particularly good and secure in because I know they are of the best quality or of the quality I wanted, but I can equally enjoy a two-dollar wooden ring from K-Mart for the same reasons. Snobbery has little to do with being well dressed; true fashion has much more to do with self-knowledge and self-expression than it does with "high fashion."

Cataloguing the Catalogues

Bless the mailman who keeps the catalogues coming day after day after day. When they first started arriving several years ago, I had the leisure time to read them. Now I am wondering how to get my name removed from the mailing lists. To alleviate the problem of what to do with the damn things, I have developed a system. I have a reference shelf for those I wish to keep as is; I clip and file useful information from others, and some I throw away immediately. If you don't decide to make a purchase from them, use them to get ideas about colors, styles, and new ways of accessorizing. But if you don't have a system, throw them away because you will never really use them.

There are basically two types of catalogues. One is from companies that sell only through mail order. The other type is sent from stores or companies that also sell their merchandise at retail stores throughout the country. Catalogues are of particular advantage to people who live where the number of stores is limited, for people who have minimal shopping time or who cannot leave home to shop. You might enjoy using catalogues at busy shopping seasons when stores are crowded, for unique items, or to stimulate your imagination. Today catalogue sales are increasing along with the rise in the cost of gasoline.

Be wary of certain catalogue companies. If they ask for cash only, do not order from them. If you have not purchased from them before and their policies are not indicated, write and ask about this and be sure you keep any statement of policy available in case you do return an item. Often what looks good in a catalogue photograph is the photography and not the merchandise. Read the description carefully, note the fabric content, the colors, and other pertinent information. Unless you are familiar with the brand and know that it fits you, you will be taking a chance in ordering merchandise that is sized; and you will have to pay the postage if you send it back. If you choose to have something monogrammed, you will not be able to return it if you are dissatisfied.

If the store sending the catalogue is nearby, call and ask if the merchandise is in the store; then, to be more certain of your purchase, you can go in and look at it. It usually takes three to four weeks for an item to be delivered. Different companies offer exactly the same merchandise at different prices and postage charges. If the merchandise is costly and could be easily damaged, you will have more difficulty dealing with an out-of-town company. Watches, jewelry, and furs should not be purchased from catalogues without keeping this fact in mind.

Hurrah for the Yellow Pages!

I agree with letting your fingers do the jogging. Since I began writing this book I have had even less time than when I thought I had no free time at all. In order to cope, I have taught myself to use and rely on the telephone, the telephone book, and store advertisements. When I want to order an advertised blouse, or duplicate an item such as a pair of the same hose, or a leotard in the same style but a new color, I feel comfortable calling the store rather than going in each time. I save all pertinent information from the sales slip and package. When calling I ask for the same salesperson who helped me previously in the store.

If you too want to follow the above approach, learn also about the store's policies. Is there a delivery charge? Some stores charge for a purchase under $10, but if you order several items from different departments, most stores will send you an inclusive package with no delivery fee. Some stores will deliver the same day you order the item, adding a service charge. When you're in a time bind this service can be important to you regardless of the additional cost. If you are not familiar with a store or don't know who carries a certain item, the telephone book lists most stores and often individual departments. Even if you plan to go into the store for your purchase, you may save valuable time by calling ahead; if the item is not in the store, ask if it can be ordered for you.

Avoiding Media Frustration

No, you shouldn't wear those pictured white silk pants if you are a size 16. And perhaps the top shown with them is the wrong color and style for you too. Seeing styles you can't wear and prices you can't afford in magazines and newspapers will naturally frustrate you. But you can use media advertising to learn about styles for the coming season. If the prices are higher than you can afford, use the ideas for your own adaptations. Look to the ads for coordinating hints and color choices. The newest ideas about what to wear are often seen in newspapers and magazines before they are available in the stores. If you keep the photographs, they can help you when you shop.

Shopping is thinking and developing skills, not just buying and paying.

13

Salespeople

How do you choose a good salesperson? This choice may make the difference between shopping success and failure.

Most salespeople will give better service if you make specific requests.

To get personalized help, you must talk about yourself.

Here's the scenario. You've made the firm decision, today's the day. Your make-up has been applied with flair, you've run your fingers through your hair for the final time. You catch a glimpse of yourself in the hall mirror. You pass your self-inspection. Even last night's dinner doesn't show on your tummy. You take a deep breath, suck in, and assure yourself a size 10 will fit. In fact, if this is to be an exceptional shopping day, you might just bring home a size 8, since the better brands are often cut fuller.

See Jane Shop. Shop Jane Shop.

On your way to the shop, you lose a bit of self-confidence as to whether you have your figure in shape. But it won't take long for your spirits to be heightened since, after all, salespeople work to make a living and they know when flattery counts the most. You arrive at the store, but the last time you were here was at least a year ago, so you take a minute to get your bearings.

Now you head right for the pantsuits. One of two things can happen at this point: either you're totally ignored and wonder if anyone works here or you're descended upon by three of the three salespeople in the department. You spend a short time studying the merchandise, and sooner or later you hear the official greeting, "May I help you?" (Nine out of ten times that will be the opener.)

You gather up a few pantsuits to try on, and before you're properly zipped and buttoned, the ooh's and ah's begin, the start of the flowery sales pitch. Through the eager salesperson's eyes, everything looks grand and custom made for you. Self-confidence is your only defense. You must be unafraid of criticism, and understand that on her first encounter with you a salesperson is probably more interested in selling merchandise than in being totally honest with you, the customer. Be assertive at this time, and make her keenly aware that you are interested in establishing a long-term shopping relationship and that you need her sincerity and guidance. Your goal is to develop a personal shopping understanding which you can count on consistently. This is really what you want. Good selling is always sincere.

Where Is the Sin in Sincere?

In Atlanta I buy most of my clothes in a small specialty shop, not only because it has the most innovative fashions in the city, but because the store owner and I have an iron-clad relationship. I relinquish being a professional shopper and enjoy her selling expertise. Her sincerity is loud and clear. She never fails to verbalize compliments when she deems them accurate. But I also have been told to "Go home and lose five pounds," or "It looks awful, take it off," or "If you like it, forget where you bought it, don't tell a person it came from my shop." I love her for her honesty.

You are responsible not only for choosing clothes, but for finding a salesperson who will take a personal interest in you. Be conscious of these criteria.

Where Is the Person in Salesperson?

How do you choose a good salesperson? This choice may make the difference between shopping success and failure. There are critical rules for making the right decision. Some salespeople in good stores are professionals, and though they don't know you, they know their merchandise and the store's policies. Chose a salesperson who will understand you and your needs, but don't expect her to read your mind. To get personalized help, you must talk about yourself. Here are some things the salesperson will need to know (and the more specific you are the better):

What item are you shopping for? (For example, "I need a beige satin shirt. I'm keeping the bride's book at a noon church wedding.")
What size are you?
Is your purchase to go with an item you now have in your wardrobe? (It is best to have the item with you.)
What brands fit you well?
What information about your lifestyle will be pertinent?
For what occasion(s) will you be wearing the purchase, and when?

Etiquette While Shopping

In selecting a salesperson, these are the things you should do and the customs you should observe:

Do not interrupt a salesperson while she is busy with another customer.
Take time to watch a salesperson with another customer, and if you like her working style, it will be worth your time to wait until she is available to work with you.
Do not be rushed and do not rush the salesperson.
When you select someone to assist you, introduce yourself. If she is not wearing a store name tag, ask her name. This personalizes your shopping relationship.
If you prefer browsing at first, request that the salesperson check with you in a brief time. Never say "I am just looking," as this is a sure way to lose contact with a helpful salesperson.

It Doesn't Hurt to Ask

Most good salespeople will give better service if you make specific requests. If you want to match clothes or accessories from another department within the store, ask for their assistance in doing this. If you are unable to find your correct size and the store has branches in this city or another, ask that they contact the other store for availability of the merchandise. (Very often a salesperson will not make this effort unless you ask. Be sure to wait with her while she makes these calls.) If you need more time to make this purchase, request that the merchandise be held for a specific time. If you need more assistance in a fitting room, you can ask for other merchandise from the selling floor. Always ask how to care for the merchandise, and make certain you understand about this. (Instructions for care of the garment must be attached to it.) Always understand the exchange and return policies of the store before your final decision, since stores vary greatly in this.

The Purchase Is Prologue

If you have completed your shopping and have been pleased with the salesperson's help, say so. If you expect to shop there again, ask for a personal business card, and be sure to give your name and telephone number and the best time to reach you if you want to be informed of related items, sales, or other events. Ask that she write down any pertinent information for your next purchase such as what you bought, the brand, size, and color. Ask that she call you if something comes into the store that is new and would add to your wardrobe. And when you are ready to make another purchase, telephone the salesperson to inquire if the merchandise is in. For best results in personal shopping, shop with the same salesperson each time you are in that store. Asking when the salesperson will be available to help you will avoid an unnecessary trip or at least save you time.

Constructive sales help may be vanishing, but is not yet extinct. It is up to you, the consumer, to develop teamwork between yourself and the salesperson and thus preserve an endangered species.

14

Store Policies and Services

Services make the difference. Most clothes can be found in many places. Choose a store that offers the best policies and gives the best service for the money you wish to spend.

Don't be passive. Knowledge of what to wear must be supplemented by knowing how to get the best service and most comfort when you shop.

Store policies differ, so be assertive and ask what the store's individual policies are.

Although it is the merchandise that first lures you into a store, take time to inquire about services and policies. Stores advertise and promote the positive policies and services they offer to the customer, and some may even neglect to inform you of their unique amenities.

It is also up to you to ask in advance rather than discover later at home that the sales slip says in very small print "This is a final sale." The phrase *caveat emptor* ("let the buyer beware") always applies, especially if you don't know the store or if you are from out of town. Although consumer protection laws may help, it is much better to take self-protective action rather than get into letters and phone calls after the fact. A gram of protection is worth a kilogram of cure.

Always Ask These Questions:

What forms of *payment* are available? (Is it cash only; specific credit cards; personal check; store charge account? Is there a late-payment charge; interest charge; 30-day, 60-day, or 90-day payment plan?)

Can you *return* merchandise? Can you return for store credit only (against other purchases), or will they actually refund your money ? Is there a specific time within which the merchandise must be returned (seven days, two weeks, etc.)? Can sale merchandise be returned? Often, if it is on sale, it is not returnable. Can furs, evening wear, jewelry, swimsuits, and undergarments be returned? There are different return policies for certain merchandise, even within the same store. Can merchandise be returned if it is damaged after wearing by factors beyond your control, such as shrinkage, fading, broken zippers, etc. Can the merchandise be returned to another branch of the same store in your own area or in another city? This is important to know when you are shopping out of town.

If you are given a gift and you want to return it without a salescheck, can you get a cash refund? If not, beware of this store for gift-giving or receiving.

When you have asked the above questions of the store, be sure you are satisfied with the answers. Recently my friend purchased a skirt and sweater for her daughter and was assured by the salesperson, with an overpowering smile, "Of course your daughter can return them." Yes, they were returnable, but only for merchandise credit, and now there is a $70 credit in a store she does not want to buy from in the future. Be very specific when you ask these questions, and write down the name of the salesperson who gives you the answer. Whether you are shopping in a small boutique or in a very large department store, you can easily ask for the name of your informant. This name is also very important to have whenever you are dealing with a large organization or bureaucracy; asking names first gets you more reliable answers. Keep the salescheck from the purchase, since most stores today will not allow returns without the receipt.

Last year I bought a blouse in New York, purchasing it in a hurry despite the sign "No Returns." When I got home to Atlanta I found one sleeve damaged. I wrote the store, but received no reply. Since I had charged the blouse on a major credit card, I called the credit company, explained the situation, and asked them to contact the store. They did and after returning the merchandise by registered mail, I was given credit. Especially if you are shopping away from home, I strongly suggest using a major credit card, since most stores do have at least one major credit card available. The no-return principle is not legitimately applied to defective merchandise, and I certainly feel it is justified in these situations to use the assistance of the company issuing your credit card.

If you are shopping at a discount, sample, or merchandise outlet opera-tion, you will probably find that its policies are cash payment and no returns. Make your selection slowly in these stores, be very sure of proper fit, and examine the merchandise carefully for any defects. If the store offers only seconds (slightly damaged or imperfect merchandise), be sure it is not the kind of defect that will get worse as a result of wearing, washing, or cleaning the item.

"Will you hold this for me?" Policies on holding merchandise differ, but ask. You may want to comparison-shop elsewhere, take time for lunch before making a decision, discuss it with someone else, or come back the next day. Ask how long the merchandise will be held, so you won't come back to find your selection sold. If you decide against the purchase, be courteous and let the store know, so they can put it back in stock.

Don't Minimize Service

Service makes the difference. Yes, some stores offer unique merchandise, but most clothes can be found in many places. Choose a store that offers the best policies and gives the best service for the money you wish to spend. In bargain stores (discount, sample, outlet), the services usually are reduced in order to give you reduced prices.

If your schedule is busy and small price differences are not too significant, you want to know the services the store will provide to save you time, and what comforts you can enjoy while shopping there. If your budget is extremely tight, services will be less significant. Cost and service usually have to be balanced against each other, although sometimes very expensive stores give poor service.

Other Services

Are *alterations* available? This saves time, but most store alterations cost more than outside private alterations. Therefore, ask the specific cost before approving the alterations. Some stores will pin the garment for you at no cost, which will enable you to alter it yourself. If the store alters your merchandise, it is responsible for the work. If you do not use their alteration department, this becomes your responsibility. If the altering is complex, use the store service. Some stores alter pants, particularly jeans, at no cost. If you buy pants or jeans in a men's store, there is usually no alteration charge.

Does the store *deliver*? Is there a charge? How quickly will you receive it? Some stores have their own delivery service, but many use a local service which can take several days to reach you. If you need the items by a specific time you might choose to pick them up yourself or take them.

Many stores, regardless of size, offer *personal shopping* for customers. If your time is limited, if you are from out of town, or if you have been invited somewhere at the last minute, this service can be a wonderful timesaver. A small store you shop in frequently should always be helpful, but larger stores often provide the customer with this personal service. Some years ago a customer came into a large department store at five o'clock from her office, dressed in a casual pantsuit, low-heeled shoes, and a short plaid jacket. She had received a call, only moments before, from a man she was dating. He asked her to be with him at a six o'clock dinner which was politically important to him. She lived forty-five minutes from downtown and had no time to return home to dress, but her office was across the street from the store. Within thirty minutes we completely dressed her from inside out. A cosmetician redid her make-up and we loaned her a long satin coat. Stores don't invite this as habit, but if they are very service-oriented they will go out of their way to please. I remember, too, the lady who called from a nearby hotel an hour before the store closed, panicked because her luggage was lost. She was in Atlanta to give a speech at seven o'clock that evening. After getting her dress and shoe size, we collected several outfits and accessories for her to choose from and delivered them to her hotel. I will always remember her appreciation for our store and our city. This was irreplaceable good will and good retailing practice. In a crisis, don't be afraid to ask for help from a store with high service standards. The worst that can happen is that they will laugh at you or just say "I'm sorry we can't (or won't) do that."

I strongly urge you to use judgment about store services and policies; in the last few years stores have begun to discontinue these because of customer abuse and loss of money. Atlanta department store president Dick Rich subscribed to the philosophy, "The customer is always right," and it would be better for consumers if stores could retain their faith in their customers.

The Best Things in Shopping Aren't Free

You pay for comfortable shopping. Although the store won't send you a bill for its services, you do pay more for your merchandise. The cost is hidden, but if you do want to shop with greater ease and comfort, it's worth what you pay for it.

Nothing is more annoying when I shop than being crammed into a tiny fitting room, without a chair, and usually without hooks for hanging my clothes or the merchandise. If I'm tired and have packages, I usually leave. Not only will I be frustrated by the room size, but I'll probably never get a good view of myself in the clothes because of poor mirrors and lighting. Buying mistakes will result from insufficient space and light.

How efficient are the salespeople? Do they give you personal attention? Feel free to ask for help, including assistance in hanging up the merchandise, bringing another size to the fitting room, getting in and out of the clothes, and deciding how things look on you. A good store has enough salespeople to give you this assistance.

Know Your Rights and Assert Them

Don't be passive. If you are unhappy with either the merchandise or the service in the store, say so. Often you must ask for the store owner or manager. I firmly believe in going to the top almost immediately. A person on the selling floor may have no authority or may pass the buck. Never take for granted that you will get satisfaction (or that you can't get satisfaction). If you want immediate action and don't want to be bothered talking to three people, you will get quicker attention from someone in authority. Most stores want to know a customer's legitimate complaints. If the person in authority is not in the store at the time, ask that person's name and reach him or her later by telephone. Be persistent.

Epilogue: Case Studies

Fashion Problem #1: Re-entering the Job Market

Identification. Ms. C. is fifty years old, brown hair, looks very young for her age, will be entering the job market for the first time in fourteen years. She wears a size 6, is five feet two, and weighs 112 pounds.

Chief Complaint. "In the last five to ten years, I have had difficulty finding clothes that are youthful, but not girlish. Because I am short and wear a small size, my selection is limited. I can't find clothes that reflect the career image I now want. I want to look my age."

History of Present Fashion Problems. "Because I haven't worked in many years, my wardrobe consists of very casual clothes. I'll be working in a law firm as receptionist for the senior partner. I've been trying to change my image, but find it very confusing, especially because of the limited clothes to choose from."

Ms. C. realizes that she thinks primarily about style in selecting her wardrobe while neglecting other issues. She pays little attention to color in selecting her ready-to-wear, and she neglects accessories that could give her the look she wants. Her clothes selection will be somewhat limited because many styles are designed for taller women.

Past History. Ms. C. has, over the years, been constantly pessimistic about her wardrobe. Because there is a limited selection for the very short woman, shopping has been frustrating. Almost all of her clothes require costly alterations. Since she has matured and wants a more sophisticated look, she has an even greater problem. She has not understood the importance of accessories in allowing styles that are attractive on her to be more flexible.

FASHION EXAMINATION

Personal. Ms. C. has a slender, well-kept figure. Her clothes do not reflect her personality, and most of the styles she has chosen are too mature or too girlish. Because she has an attractive figure for clothes, she can look smart in many styles. She does not make enough use of correct shoe heel height or the right colors and styles to give her a taller appearance. Most importantly, she lacks knowledge of the right use of accessories.

Closet. Some of the clothes she has will be too casual for her new job. However, she has some separates that can be coordinated with some new garments to adapt them for work. She has included too many colors and patterns in her wardrobe, which limits the use of accessories because shoes and purses are often the wrong color, scarves and jewelry are the wrong look for her ready-to-wear. She has not updated her wardrobe with newer fashion looks, which is an important issue for an on-the-job wardrobe.

DIAGNOSIS AND ANALYSIS

Psychological. Ms. C. needs more understanding of a flexible wardrobe. She must learn to appreciate the positive features of her figure. She also must get individual help during her shopping to learn new clothes and accessory ideas and techniques.

Appearance. Not updated. Does not choose clothes or use accessories that add height.

Closet. She will have to replace some of her clothes and accessories with recent fashion looks. Needs assistance to coordinate her blouses and some sweaters with new additions. Closet should be organized by clothes categories.

PLAN AND PURCHASES

We discussed her activities in her new career, including the clothes she would need, and the need for fabrics that would remain attractive after many hours of sitting at her desk. We reviewed the use of accessories and approaches to color in both her clothes and accessories. We agreed that I would work with her to coordinate her fall wardrobe for the office. We would decide what clothes she presently had that would be functional and what additional purchases she would need to make. We began selecting clothes together, and we later agreed I would make a list of specific items she could purchase on her own. We also agreed that twice each season I would consult with her again.

Because navy was her favorite color and was abundant in her present wardrobe, we included it as a major basic color for her new wardrobe. We added cream, rust, and powder-blue. These colors would not be seasonal and would be easy to accessorize.

For *outerwear,* we selected the following:

Cream gabardine blazer
Tan trench raincoat (zip-out lining)
Heavy wool multicolor coat sweater (navy with rusts and cream)

These items will give enough warmth for her climate. They will be easy to coordinate with the other items in her wardrobe, and will be very suitable for the office.

In *skirts and slacks* we selected:

Navy and cream wool tweed slacks (to wear with cream blazer)
Navy gabardine slacks
Cream gabardine skirt
Rust corduroy skirt
Navy flannel skirt

These bottoms will coordinate with all of the tops we chose as well as with the outerwear. They can give both a suited look or a coordinated separates look. Though we included pants, she will seldom wear them to the office. The fabric selections will show a minimal amount of wrinkling.

Our *blouse and sweater* selections were:

Powder-blue silky shirt, long sleeve
Powder-blue silky shirt, three-quarter sleeve
Cream pattern-on-pattern long-sleeved silk shirt
Navy and rust print voile shirt
Rust wool-knit tailored shirt (very casual)
Navy wool vest sweater
Cream cowl-neck sweater
Powder-blue cowl-neck sweater

We chose two *dresses*:

Basic navy flannel dress that can be layered underneath with blouses or sweaters
Beige silk-blend two-piece dress that can easily be worn from the office out for the evening

Accessories

Shoes. Brown high-heeled suede pump; beige leather pump, high stacked heel; brown high-heeled leather sport shoe.
Purses. Dark brown leather pouch with handles; brown patterned clutch.
Jewelry. Tortoise shell bracelets — one wide, one narrow bangle; gold mesh bracelet; long gold bar pins (two); small gold pins (two); large wooden pin; earrings (three pair in different shapes); strand of small wooden beads, 30-inch; tortoise shell choker; gold chains — one very thin, the other heavier, both 18-inch.

Additional accessories

Navy leather belt
Brown suede belt
Silk flowers
Navy velvet vest
Scarves — two solid, one print.

It took us approximately four months to complete this wardrobe. Though we concentrated on fall and winter clothes, many of the things we chose could be worn year-round.

Fashion Problem #2: New Life, Leaving Job

Identification. Ms. G. is fifty-nine years old, has dark hair with some gray. She is five feet four inches, wears a size 16, and weighs 158 pounds. Ms. G. has worked most of her adult life as a hospital dietitian. She is retiring and will begin an active community life.

Chief Complaint. "For twenty-nine years I've worn a uniform every day on the job. My clothes budget will be limited, but I want to start a wardrobe that has a complete new look. I want to include as many as possible of the clothes I have worn while not working."

History of Present Fashion Problem. Ms. G. has begun looking for clothes on her own, but seems to shop and shop without buying anything. She is not sure what type of clothes she really wants, and does not know which styles and colors look best on her. Because her budget is limited, she is very price conscious. She does not know how to establish priorities, or in which wardrobe areas to spend her money.

Past History. Because Ms. G. is overweight she is difficult to fit. She has not concentrated on manufacturers that style for a full figure, and has chosen inappropriate colors for her size. She has bought too many patterned designs that not only add apparent weight, but make her wardrobe difficult to accessorize.

FASHION EXAMINATION

Personal. Ms. G. has an attractive face and is very neat in her appearance, but has not found a look in her clothes that will accentuate her positive features. She has lovely long fingers but does not wear much jewelry on her fingers or at her wrist. The height of her shoes does not give her figure a taller, longer look. She tends to emphasize color around her stomach, hips, and thighs but not around her face, therefore drawing attention where she does not mean to.

Closet. Her wardrobe is very small, because of her minimal needs during her work career. Most of the clothes she now has will need to be either updated or accessorized for more flexibility in her new wardrobe.

DIAGNOSIS AND ANALYSIS

Psychological. Must learn how to shop, instead of just spending time in stores. This will require her learning a plan, and learning how to make decisions to implement it. She requires support and guidance in beginning a wardrobe, and understanding about how to add to it each season.

Appearance. Ms. G's look is not updated. She has not added height to her figure or minimized figure width by proper use of style and color.

Closet. Her closet is not set up for the clothes we will purchase. Reorganization is needed to make her clothes accessible and easier to mix, change, and vary.

PLAN AND PURCHASES

We discussed her budget, which will be approximately $600 for her spring and summer wardrobe. She expects to be very active in a local garden club, and will attend a college enrichment program once a week. She will need clothes for these activities and more casual ones for her unplanned time.

For *outerwear* we selected the following:

Navy linen jacket, unconstructed in style, which can be worn with or without the self belt
Wheat crocheted cardigan sweater, short sleeves

The jacket can be worn beginning in April until the weather turns very hot. The sweater can be worn year-round with either a long-sleeved blouse underneath or with short-sleeve tops as the weather becomes warmer.

In *skirts and slacks* we selected:

Navy linen slacks
Navy cotton slacks
Camel linen slacks
Camel challis skirt with soft A-line

These bottoms can be worn either with tops alone or with the jacket for a suited look. The cotton slacks and challis skirt can both be worn through spring, summer, and late fall.

Our *tops* selections were:

Beige crocheted long-sleeved top, V-neckline
Cream short-sleeved silky V-neck top, camel and beige trim at neckline
Cream short-sleeved silky V-neck top, camel and jade-green trim at neckline
White eyelet blouse, long sleeve
Navy voile blouse, long sleeve
Powder-blue loose T-shirt, short sleeve

The tops can be coordinated with all the bottoms, and can be layered in cooler weather.

We added one *dress*:

Navy crepe with matching jacket, trimmed with camel at collar and cuffs

This dress can be worn year-round. It can give the effect of a jumper worn with a blouse underneath and no jacket. The fabric and style are appropriate for both daytime and evening.

Accessories

Shoes. Navy high-heeled leather pump; navy stacked-heel pant shoe; camel high-heeled leather sandal, which can be worn casual or dressy; navy canvas and straw espadrille.

Purses. Camel leather bag for daytime, large; navy leather envelope for day or night, small.

Jewelry. White button earrings, white loops; white beads, choker length; ivory beads, 18 inches; small enamel pins (two); gold bracelets (two); silver bracelet, wide; rings — two enamel, one gold, one silver.

Additional accessories

Challis scarves, two with vivid prints
Cream silk rosebuds

We spent $692 for Ms. G's spring and summer wardrobe. Many of the clothes and accessories we chose can easily be worn in fall and winter. I kept the colors very limited, and suggested we add mauve and wine for fall and winter. Except for the canvas and straw shoe, the shoes and purses can be worn year-round.

Fashion Problem #3: Extended Travel

Identification. Ms. R. is twenty-seven years old, has very long bright red hair. She is five feet five, weighs 127 pounds, and wears a size 10.

Fashion Problem. She will be traveling in Europe for six weeks as part of an art study group. The tour requests one piece of luggage per person, and she will be responsible in most places for carrying it herself. Though most of her time will be spent in Paris, she will be taking some short side trips. She will be traveling in April and May, and will need clothes that are easy to care for and appropriate for working, sightseeing, and evening entertainment.

DIAGNOSIS AND ANALYSIS

Psychological. Ms. R. is accustomed to having a lot of clothes to choose from, but a limiting luggage allowance will create selection problems she is not ready for. She does not yet have knowledge needed to make her traveling wardrobe innovative by using accessories and interchanging her separates.

Appearance. Very casual in her appearance, Ms. R. is most comfortable in pants. Her main objective in dressing is to be comfortable.

Closet. Restricted choice is the problem for her trip. A number of the garments she already has can be worn on the trip. Because of the possibility of cool and rainy weather, she will need to add outerwear and warm clothes. She does not have comfortable shoes for walking.

PLAN AND PURCHASES

Her current accessories are minimal. In order to stretch her wardrobe while traveling, we must put emphasis on new and updated accessory additions. She wants to be sure that the clothes we choose for the trip will also work well with her present wardrobe when she returns. We coordinated her travel clothes so that they could be layered for warmth and versatility.

For *outerwear* we selected the following:

Red quilted waterproof reversible zip-front jacket
Beige trenchcoat with zip-out lining
Red velour sweatshirt, washable

These will give her warmth and rain protection. Red is her favorite color.

In *skirts and pants* we added to her present wardrobe:

Red corduroy skirt, washable
Red corduroy pants, washable
Camel polyester and wool gabardine pants, washable
Camel wool blend pantsuit, soft and washable

She will include three pair of blue jeans from her present wardrobe. The corduroy skirt, gabardine pants, and camel pantsuit are styles that can be dressed up for going out in the evening.

Our *blouse and sweater* selections were:

Cream polyester and silk shirt, washable
Navy and red satin-polyester print long-sleeved shirt, washable
Cotton long-sleeved cowl-neck T-shirts — one beige and one red (from present wardrobe)
White wool-blend cable-knit heavy sweater, washable
Red, navy, and beige striped V-neck sweater, a washable blend (from present wardrobe)

Accessories

Shoes. Brown leather lace-up walking shoes; brown leather ankle-high pant boot (from present wardrobe); brown leather pump, a good look for pants and skirts (daytime or evening).

Purse. Large brown leather drawstring pouch, which also serves as an overnight bag for weekend side trips; beige patterned canvas clutch, small.

Jewelry. Gold neckwire, with three alternate drops to hang from it; gold medium-weight chain; earrings — two casual pair, one dressy pair (from present wardrobe); two watches (from present wardrobe); bracelets — two silver, one wooden; rings (from present wardrobe).

Additional accessories

Red vinyl rain hat
Beige folding umbrella
Navy and brown striped wool cap
Scarves — three patterned, one solid
Wool mittens — one pair red, one pair brown
Red and navy paisley velvet vest, reversible to solid navy
Brown leather and suede belt

Other

Nightgowns (two)
Jersey robe, washable
White slippers, foldable and soft
Pantyhose (four pair)
Knee socks (two pair)
Underwear
Suitcase — Navy canvas, soft-sided, lightweight and expandable with zip pockets inside and outside

Because of the color and fabric combinations, all of these clothes were easy to interchange. Because of various fabric weights, the garments will be suitable for most weather conditions and easy to layer. The fabrics are easy to care for. The accessories, especially the jewelry, scarves, and vest, give great flexibility to the ready-to-wear.

Fashion Problem #4: Changing Image

Identification. The client is Mrs. M, fifty-five years old, gray-haired, attractive, a freelance writer. She wears sizes 12 and 14, is five feet five, and weighs 145 pounds. She travels a great deal both personally and professionally.

Chief Complaint. "My wardrobe has too much, has no color coordination, and is difficult to use for traveling. On top of that, it doesn't reflect my personality, and has no image. I aspire to have a certain look, but have no idea what that image should be. I want to say something about myself through my clothes."

History of Present Fashion Problem. During a fifteen-year career, Mrs. M bought at random what she liked at the moment she was shopping. There was no overall wardrobe plan. Her selections primarily reflected her family's preferences and attitudes rather than her own. She automatically bought to please others rather than herself.

She did not know how to integrate her work clothes and leisure clothes. During her travels she enjoyed buying sprees, but almost all of her purchases had no place in her wardrobe and she rarely wore them. For example, when traveling in Europe, she bought heavy wool sweaters and skirts that were wonderfully attractive, but much too heavy to wear in the mild southern climate back home. Many purchases were skirts, which she rarely wore since she feels much more comfortable in slacks for casual wearing.

Past History. Born into a rich family, as a child Mrs. M was not taught any responsibility for her own clothes selections. She was given a great variety of clothes and never learned to distinguish between basic and frivolous items. During adolescence she had little self-confidence and required her mother's (and later her husband's) approval before purchasing.Therefore, she usually bought what they liked and not what she felt comfortable and attractive in. She never had to conform to a clothes budget and, consequently, did not have to plan purchases and restrict quantity.

FASHION EXAMINATION

Personal. Mrs. M is neat and well groomed. She has a very fresh and peppy look and personality. Her short gray hair has a very distinct look of its own. She has a nice bust, but is thick through her waist and stomach, and has large legs and thighs. She was wearing a bright kelly green knit pantsuit, matching green and white striped knit blouse, green shoes, and a beige purse. Her overall look was matronly. The pantsuit was an uninteresting polyester three-piece knit. Its self-trim and buttons allowed little chance for accessorizing and personalizing. Her shoes and purse had no pizzaz.

Closet. Her closet was filled to capacity both with new clothes and clothes she had saved for fifteen years. The latter were in good condition, but outdated in style. The jackets were too long, the skirts and dresses were old shapes and much too short, and the pants had either very full legs or were tapered pedalpushers.

Some of Mrs. M's more recent purchases were too matronly, including Ultra Suede jacket dresses, polyester pants, and pantsuits. Her choice of color was much too broad, since the colors had no relationship to each other and confused her. Her accessories were outdated too. Purses were the wrong shape, shoes had high narrow heels, which did not have an updated look. Her costume jewelry was much too large and ornate. She had not purchased any costume jewelry in the last three years. She had only one bracelet, bulky enough to injure one's wrist, and it was easy to see why she never wore it.

DIAGNOSIS AND ANALYSIS

Psychological. Lack of self-confidence, desire to please family rather than herself. No planning ahead. No recognition of special travel needs. No idea what fabrics pack easily and do not wrinkle.

Appearance. Matronly. Too broad a choice of color. Brights worn below the waist accentuate her hips, thighs, and legs.

Closet. She keeps unworn and out-of-style clothes. Her closet needs organization.

PLANS AND PURCHASES

We discussed the problems we had identified together, and the fact that she would go through a learning process lasting several months. I would explain my thinking as we went along and she would integrate this with her own values and view of herself. For example, I explained how she unintentionally accentuated her hips, and I recommended wearing light and bright colors above the waist and dark solid colors below the waist. She should not call attention to her hips. We began working on a fall-winter wardrobe and eliminated everything in her present wardrobe except the following items: one pair of brown leather boots, one pair of navy low stacked-heel casual shoes, one pair of navy wool gabardine slacks, three sweaters (navy, powder-blue, rose), and four blouses of the same color family as the sweaters, including two solids and two prints. We agreed I would purchase the continuation of her wardrobe by picking out and sending items for her approval and fit. I asked that she make no purchase without my assistance until we both felt she had learned enough about buying her own wardrobe.

We selected the basic colors of navy, gray, and wine, partly because they added importance to her gray hair (one of her strongest and most attractive physical features). These colors also would be easy and right to wear wherever she traveled and whatever the climate, since they are not seasonal and allow for a great deal of color coordinating.

For *outerwear,* we selected the following:

Gray velvet blazer
Wine soft-leather coat
Beige raincoat
Navy peajacket

These items are comfortable to wear when traveling. They are not difficult to pack, and such styles can be used for either casual or dressy wear. The raincoat and blazer can be dressed up easily for evening. The four separate items could be adapted to various climates, and all can be worn with sweaters underneath if necessary for colder weather.

In *skirts and slacks,* we selected:

Navy wool gabardine slacks (in a more casual style than those already in her wardrobe)
Gray flannel slacks
Black matte jersey slacks
Gray wool long skirt
Navy wool jersey two-piece dress
Gray and wine small-check skirt

These styles would work well in the daytime or evening. The colors and styles would always look smart with the coats and jackets we chose, and would easily coordinate with the tops in her wardrobe.

Our *blouse and sweater* selections were:

Fuchsia long-sleeved silk blouse
Blush-pink long-sleeved silk blouse
Wine and navy print voile long-sleeved blouse
White silk pattern-on-pattern long-sleeved silk blouse
Wine cashmere cowl-neck sweater
Beige wool long-sleeve pullover
Navy wool cardigan

Each of the blouses and sweaters could be combined together, and all of them are wearable with the bottoms we chose and can be worn daytime or evening.

Accessories

Shoes. Navy suede sandal; pewter leather pump; gray suede low stacked heel; black silk sandal.
Purses. Pewter large soft-leather pouch; gray leather clutch.
Jewelry. Two wooden bangle bracelets; sterling silver and wood bangle bracelet; wine wooden bangle bracelet; sterling silver neckband with tiger's eye pendant; pierced earrings (three pair); amber and gold stick pin.

We were easily able to keep the shoes and purses limited, but appropriate for all occasions. This made the accessories convenient for traveling and also easy to interchange. The jewelry pieces were not seasonal and were effective worn alone or combined with each other. I also wanted to integrate gold and silver with the clothes, so we added a a silver metal belt and a narrow navy leather one with gold buckle to be worn with skirts and slacks. A gray wool muffler worn around the shoulders or with the blazer and peajacket also tied the outfits together.

We achieved a flexible wardrobe and one that will be easy to add to next season.

Glossary

Active sportswear. Clothes or uniforms worn for active participation in a sport such as tennis or golf, as distinguished from sportswear or leisure clothes.

Armoire (arm-*wahr*). A large wardrobe or cabinet which can be used for holding or storing clothes. Some have shelves and drawers, others have hanging space only. A mirror can be attached to the inside or outside of the armoire door, which may have a lock.

Attache case (atta-*shay*). Briefcase used for carrying business papers, etc.

Basic. An item that is necessary in your wardrobe, such as a purse. Also, a style that is basic or classic in your wardrobe, such as a blazer.

Bias cut. A method of cutting a fabric at an angle to the weave. A bias-cut silhouette means a total effect in which the clothing falls and drapes gracefully on the body.

Blouson (*blues*-on). A top (shirt, blouse, sweater, or jacket) with a drawstring or elastic at the waistline or hips. Some dress styles have an elastic inset or drawstring at the waist to achieve a blouson effect, which is soft and blousy.

Caftan. A floor-length, full garment in a soft fabric, worn hanging loose or tied with a soft sash. The sleeves are long and full. A popular style for at-home wear, and worn frequently by overweight women.

Classic. A style in clothes and accessories, usually in simple taste, that continues for many years in spite of changing fashions. A blazer, trenchcoat, and the leather pump are classics.

Couture (koo-*toor*). Clothing custom-made by a fashion designer. Usually one-of-a-kind and often made to order.

Dirndl. A dress or skirt softly gathered or pleated at the waistline, giving a rounded shape to the garment.

Dolman sleeve. A sleeve fitted at the shoulder and extending almost to the waistline to give a cape-like effect. The sleeve can fit loose or snug at the wrist.

Fad. A current fashion or accessory, or a current way of wearing a style. The opposite of classic, but could become so. Shell necklaces were a fad of the early 70's. Faddish is the adjective.

Fill-ins. Items added to your existing wardrobe for completeness or replacement. Buying an additional pair of black leather shoes in a season is filling in your shoe wardrobe with a necessary item.

High-styled. Dramatic or unusual; effect achieved by a garment or accessory that is styled with unusual lines. A person who dresses in high style often wears clothes that call attention, or wears them in an individualistic way.

Layered. A look achieved by wearing garments over one another. A jacket worn over a sweater and vest is an example of layering.

Lingerie straps. Tiny snap straps of ribbon, lace, or fabric sewn into the shoulder of a garment to hold bra straps in place.

Novelty. A fashion or accessory that is new or unusual and not a necessary or basic item in your wardrobe. Extras, such as a fun fur jacket or red vinyl boots, are novelty items. A basic item worn in an unconventional way can become a novelty. A basic scarf worn as a headband is worn as a novelty.

Obi. A broad sash in either a solid or pattern fabric, first worn by Japanese men and women.

Pacific cloth. A soft cloth or fabric treated to prevent silver from tarnishing (turning dull and losing its shine).

Peasant look. A dress, blouse, or skirt in a soft solid or print fabric. The neckline is usually scooped, often elasticized and trimmed in lace or appliqué. The sleeves are either short and puffed, or long and full. The skirt is tiered or flounced.

Portfolio. A flat case for holding loose papers, drawings, etc.

Ready-to-wear. Clothes that are already made when you select them and are made in some volume and various sizes. Opposed to those that are custom made to your order, or on a one-of-a-kind scale (see Couture).

Spot cleaning. A method of removing a specific spot or spots from a garment. For best results it is done on the reverse side of the fabric first, using a clean *white* cloth, a Q-tip, or a cotton swab to apply the spot remover.

Trenchcoat. Traditionally a cotton poplin raincoat in beige, which is double-breasted with a military collar, epaulets, and a self-belt pulled tight at the waist. The style was originally worn by officers in World War I trench warfare. Trenchcoat adaptations are available in an assortment of fabrics and colors.

Appendix: Personal Diary

On these pages enter your pertinent wardrobe and shopping information. Refer to them often and use the blank pages to add other information that will make dressing easier for you.

Basic Garments in Your Present Wardrobe

Colors in Your Present Wardrobe, Colors You Will Add

Clothes and Accessories to be Purchased

Where You Have Shopped (Name of Store, Etc.)

Names of Salespeople (List by Store)

Brand Names (Those You Like, Those That Fit Well, Etc.)

Sizes of Garments

Prices of Garments

Garment Information (Care Instructions, Fabric Content, Etc.)

Index